To the greatest old mate anyone could ever wish for! Thanks for sharing my life journey, John

DIARY OF A TOE RAG

A Childhood Memoir from Harlesden to Hemel Hempstead through the 1950s

Steve Riches

Diary of a Toe Rag

by

Steve Riches

Copyright 2018 Steve Riches

All rights reserved. No part of this publication may be reproduced, stored in a retrieval system or transmitted in any form or by any means electronic, mechanical, audio, visual or otherwise, without prior permission of the copyright owner (steveriches@virginmedia.com). Nor can it be circulated in any form of binding or cover other than that in which it is published and without similar conditions including this condition being imposed on the subsequent purchaser.

ISBN: 978-1-9164413-0-9

Copy edited by Ian Large

Cover design by Jag Lall

Front cover: The author, aged four, in the back garden of 26 Benchleys Road, Hemel Hempstead.

This book is produced by Granda Publishing in conjunction with **WRITERSWORLD**, and is produced entirely in the UK. It is available to order from most bookshops in the United Kingdom, and is also globally available via UK based Internet book retailers.

WRITERSWORLD

2 Bear Close Flats, Bear Close, Woodstock

Oxfordshire, OX20 1JX, England

01993 812500

+44 1993 812500

www.writersworld.co.uk

The text pages of this book are produced via an independent certification process that ensures the trees from which the paper is produced come from well managed sources that exclude the risk of using illegally logged timber while leaving options to use post-consumer recycled paper as well.

Dedication

To my wonderful, wonderful grandchildren:

Ben and Chloe, Edward and Trixie.

Written for you, so you know how it was for me.

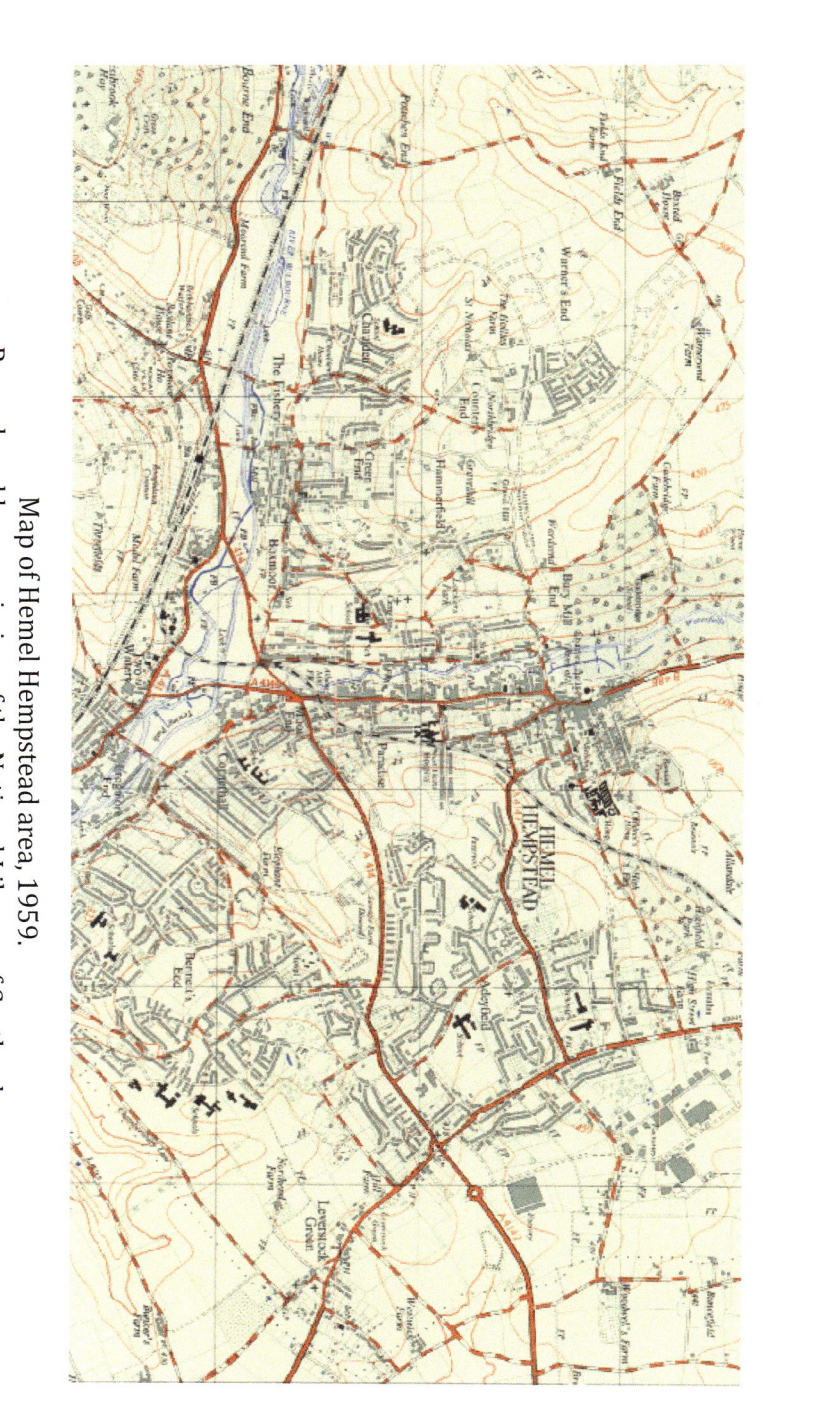

Map of Hemel Hempstead area, 1959.
Reproduced by permission of the National Library of Scotland.

Contents

	Introduction	7
	How It All Began	8
1	Rented Rooms In Springwell Avenue	9
2	Chance Of A Lifetime	17
3	And We're Off	22
4	Hello Infant School	28
5	On The Street Where You Live	36
6	Moving On	42
7	Home And Away Matches	49
8	On The Other Side	60
9	Holidays	71
10	Christmas & Co	80
11	Up To The Juniors	91
12	Away From School	99
13	The World Of Reading	104
14	Boys And Girls Come Out To Play	111
15	Happy Parenting	116
16	Money, Money, Money	124
17	Politics And Religion	128
18	Starting Work	132
19	Football Crazy	136
20	School Trips	143
21	Having A Lovely Time	150
22	Plenty To Report	156
23	Presents By Post	162
24	Granda And Colin	165
25	...And The Ending	169

Introduction

I have chosen to share my childhood with whoever wants to read the following pages, having originally set out to tell my story for the sole benefit of my grandchildren.

Not all of my childhood, just the part of it from birth to leaving junior school.

It encompasses the years 1950-1962, years of monumental change in post-war England.

It's the very simplest of books, all about me and my life. My life on a burgeoning council estate within the new town of Hemel Hempstead after my parents took the opportunity they were given to leave behind the Harlesden part of a London wrecked by the Second World War.

It's a personal social history, if it needs classifying.

Did I have an idyllic childhood? No idea. I only had the one, how do I know?

Be your own judge. All I can do is tell it as best I can.

The information within comes from two sources, both of them fallible. My memory and my research. That's all.

I make no apology for any inaccuracies, offences caused or for being self-indulgent like I never have before.

What follows is how it was for me all those years ago.

Steve Riches, 2018

How It All Began

I started life being routinely suspended about three feet above piles of dog shit.

OK, it's not a real first-up memory as such, seeing as I was tinier than a toddler, but it's as representative of my roots as it gets, or so I'm told. The nearest I can manage.

I was suspended, safely and securely as it happens, in a second-hand Silver Cross pram and daily waltzed around pet-too-friendly Roundwood Park, affectionately known by locals as Dog Shit Alley.

It was proudly steered, never dragged, around the massed ranks of canine deposits by my mum, dressed the same as all the other mums in shoes that hurt, dull beige raincoats tightly belted around wasp-like waists, and bright dinner lady headscarves struggling to enslave long flowing locks with frayed ends.

Each of them puffed Player's Weights while aiming their own second-hand Silver Cross they couldn't really afford, complete with an enclosed infant enveloped in hand-me-downs from who-cares-where.

They paused to squat on the slats of the polished wooden roundabout, crossed their seamed stockinged legs, shared dreams none of them would ever realise and drew on more fags via bright red lips as they twirled gently round and round in Roundwood Park.

It was an oasis, an escape from reality while the menfolk were at work in impossibly boring jobs rebuilding the country. That's how it was.

Harlesden, London NW10. 1950.

The whole place was shit. The Germans were to blame.

"Bombed us, bleedin' Germans. Murdering Germans. Bombed women and children. Bugger 'em all." That's what Granda said.

Granda knew everything in the whole world.

1
Rented Rooms In Springwell Avenue

Granda lived with Nanny just up the road from Roundwood Park, at No. 11 Springwell Avenue.

Their son, John, shared the accommodation with his wife, Joyce.

All the skint newly-weds lived with parents in 1950, in the September of which I joined the little wrinkly ranks, and John and Joyce became Dad and Mum after 17 months of marriage.

It was on the 24th that I disturbed the scales to the extent of 8lb 4oz in the Central Middlesex Hospital (always known as Park Royal Hospital because that's where it was), right by the Guinness Brewery. Cheers all round.

I was named Stephen Frederick after each of my grandfathers, as was the fashion. A coin was tossed to decide which way round. Mum won.

And so to Springwell for me, a road in which all the inhabitants lived in rented rooms, all sharing a front door to near-identical three-storey Victorian premises with total strangers.

Those very rooms have since magically morphed into 'flats' or, even more recently, 'apartments'. Back then, people told it how it really was: rented rooms from a never-seen private landlord.

Everyone hated their landlord, often for very good reasons of over-pricing, neglect, or both and 82 per cent of north London residents had one.

Once-hapless Harlesden, along with next-door Willesden, is now perceived as 'a leafy suburb' for no other reason than the continued presence of a few aged trees whose gnarled roots are spewing under then upwards to buckle the pavements and make modern Silver Cross

9

manoeuvring a bit more slalom-like for assorted East European nannies employed by the rich.

They, too, pause to puff in Roundwood Park (now beautifully landscaped and clean), fingering their smartphones and talking nonsense, as if unconsciously turning the clock back to Mum's young days.

For all its faults, and it still has many, Harlesden bears no scars of the bomb site it still was in 1950, then a harsh reminder that the area was pounded by Hermann Goering's Luftwaffe from September 1940 to June 1941.

As part of their destruction of a third of London's buildings, the Germans' Dorniers, Junkers and Heinkel aircraft bombed the local Heinz factory and Hippodrome Theatre, wrecked houses in and around Springwell Avenue and even dropped incendiary bombs (and a lone parachute mine) on the nearby cemetery. Real overkill.

In all, The Blitz claimed 28,556 innocent civilian lives in London. A similar number were severely injured.

Granda never forgot. Never.

And he never forgot his good fortune that he was too old (42) and his son too young (15) to be called up for military service when World War Two began at 11.15am on September 3, 1939, two days after the Germans invaded Poland.

Granda and Nanny

Granda was Frederick Charles Riches, born in February 1897 in his mother Edith's bedroom somewhere in Paddington, London.

He was never more precise than that, never spoke of his background, never talked about parents or siblings and became instantly grumpy if those subjects cropped up. So they didn't.

He did reveal, however, that he signed on the line as a volunteer with other Harlesden lads in order to fight in the First World War, which he and his contemporaries unfailingly referred to as the Great War.

Each and every one of them was totally ignorant of any sort of reality when they joined up at Paddington Recruiting Station. They had no idea where they were going, why they were going or what they were going to do when they got there.

They got there in late 1915 after a 13-week training regime which involved lots of PE and even more of being told what to do without question. On top of that, learning how to point a Lee-Enfield 0.303-inch rifle in the general direction of those who were pointing a Mauser Gewehr 98 back at them.

Granda's mates were killed somewhere in France, probably during the Big Push on the Somme, which started on July 1, 1916. He survived to be captured and, until repatriation in November 1918, was incarcerated as a PoW somewhere in Belgium, though he couldn't be sure exactly where and never bothered to find out afterwards. As far as we knew.

His was a classic case of Don't Mention The War. I got lucky, my mates got killed and all my hair fell out with shock. That's all for now, folks. I got a job as a postman when I got home.

Every now and then, and with no obvious prompting, Granda would burst into "eins, zwei, drei, vier, funf, sechs, sieben, acht, neun, zehn" by way of proving he'd been the only bald London postman of 1919 who could count to 10 in German and therefore hadn't totally wasted his time being banged up and half-starved in war-ravaged Belgium.

He also knew German card games like skat, a rummy-type game for three players using only 32 cards which was taught him by the bored prison guards, whoever and wherever they were.

One thing's for sure. It was the only time in his life he went abroad.

Life for Granda most days in the early 1950s began as it had when he started there in 1919, with a 20-minute stroll in his navy blue uniform before clocking on at the General Post Office's Willesden Sorting Office in Station Road.

He pulled on a matching peaked cap, knotted his tie and collected a sack of mail to strap on to the special carrier rack at the front of his sturdy red bicycle, ready for a round trip of at least 10 miles.

He would tell everyone how he got the sack every day, then laugh loudly. It was funny the first few dozen times.

He knew every street and apparently every resident's name in his designated delivery patch of London, which covered the rougher parts of Paddington and the posher parts of Mayfair. He told us he delivered to the actor Kenneth More and a couple of the singing Beverley Sisters.

I never knew if he really did, but I was proud of the Imperial Service Medal he got by way of reward when he eventually clocked up 40 years of poking things through people's letterboxes, famous or not.

Granda was a sizeable bloke, 5ft 10ins in his much-darned thick

11

woollen socks, his chest puffed out, his back straight, rotund and ruddy like a farmer, though he'd never seen one.

Off duty, he dressed in dark bell-bottomed trousers with a thick brown leather belt wrapped around the waist despite the absence of belt loops and the presence of thick grey braces. The collarless white shirt was always open-necked, even when wearing his dark grey jacket with the huge lapels and matching flat cap. Every man wore a flat cap.

On the handful of occasions I saw him wearing his only (striped) suit, he'd wear a jumper with the tie as though to help cover it up. As though non-uniform ties weren't for men like him. And they probably were not.

His black leather shoes shone brightly, a trusted combination of Kiwi Shoe Polish and spit. The bows of the laces on each foot were tied to match precisely.

He looked huge when stripped to the waist as I watched him in front of the kitchen mirror wielding his trusty razor. Lathered up from the frothy Cussons soap on his badger bristle brush, he'd drag the Gillette Rocket down his face in even strokes, then swirl the razor around in the hot water in his chipped enamel mug on the windowsill before pulling it upwards this time, using his index finger to push the end of his nose skywards so he didn't miss a bit.

Always be clean shaven, there's no excuse being unwashed or scruffy, he'd tell me, drying the Rocket on a tea towel before it touched down until tomorrow in its little brown leather pouch alongside the wooden bread bin on a shelf above the stove.

Nanny was Ellen. Just Ellen. No middle name. Born in London and two years older than Granda. If she stood up really straight, which she rarely did, she might have reached 4ft 10ins, at a push.

Like Granda, her past was not so much shrouded in mystery as completely unknown. It was as though they had some sort of pact. Or even a secret too terrible to share with others, a thought I guiltily harboured as a kid.

My favourite theory was her being a murderer. She'd had a terrible time in the workhouse, regularly beaten and almost starved to death. One night, she'd got her hands on a bread knife and stabbed the workhouse master through the heart just as he raised his whip to her for the umpteenth time. Blood splattered everywhere and everyone, of course.

In the commotion that followed, she fled into the darkness. How she met Granda is less clear in the imagination. But they both agreed to say nothing about their respective pasts for the rest of their lives.

That'll have to do.

Back in the proper world, things were rather more realistic.

At some unearthly hour, six days a week, no matter what the weather, Nanny silently took her rusting but faithful old Elswick Roadster out from the downstairs porch in Springwell Avenue, taking care to make no noise as she lifted the latch on the front gate.

She clambered on the wrinkled leather saddle and cycled the five miles through Kensal Rise along the Harrow Road and Edgware Road to Oxford Street.

There she was let in through a rear basement door to scrub the floors of Selfridges, a department store so luxurious she never even dreamed of having any of the contents. Not once in her life did she enter the shop through the front doors, as a customer.

For all that she was paid bugger-all a week, said Granda. I assumed that wasn't very much.

She always wore a felt hat like a flowerpot with a pin stuck in it for no apparent reason and nothing more inspiring than clumpy lace-up boots and heavy clothes that were darker than soot. She carried the same black leather shopping bag that had straps so long it flirted with the pavement.

When Granda spoke, she listened, then maybe joined in. The only time she ever spoke first was to tell him his tea was ready. That's how it was.

She'd bring him a discoloured dessert spoon, the Friar Tuck salt pot (a small pottery monk with a hole in his head) and a neatly-folded white cotton handkerchief by way of a napkin. She fetched big dollops of stew and suet dumplings in a floral china bowl with a hunk of crusty white bread heavily buttered and positioned on the bare oak table alongside it.

Then she'd reappear with a bowl for herself. Not even half the size, no bread. Every night.

I never ever saw a flicker of affection between them as they sat at that table for hours listening to the Light Programme on the Pye wireless set, drinking endless knitted-cosy-covered pots of thick yellowy Typhoo tea, Granda tipping his from cup into saucer and slurping it down like a cat. Two sugars each, a splash of milk and don't forget to warm the pot.

At regular intervals, he'd open his battered tobacco tin, pluck out a few strands of Golden Virginia and lay them neatly on top of a green Rizla cigarette paper.

He'd roll up the package with his nicotine-stained podgy fingers, lick the glued edge to secure it, light with a match and lean backwards as he inhaled, occasionally passing it over to Nanny so she could have a puff, but never a cigarette of her own.

As the embers of the coal fire in front of them died down, so would another day.

First Thoughts

Most of my very earliest memories are not of my parents, but of Granda and Nanny in our rooms, our territory being the first floor of No. 11 with its two bedrooms, bathroom, toilet, dining room, front room and kitchen.

Above them was the attic room, cold and dark like a neglected garden shed in winter, cobwebs dangling in the gentle draught and dust.

I had it all to myself. My home for three years and a bit.

I can see now the horrible wooden rocking horse with its barrel-like belly and scratchy mane, stabled on the landing outside my door as though guarding the steepest of creaking stairs just beyond. I was lifted on and off the thing until the screaming made them stop.

I'd steer my little blue pedal car along the hallway lino towards the kitchen until Nanny stepped in the way to prevent me crashing into the stove, where giant gloomy grey pots sat permanently and precariously, their innards gently bubbling with stew and vegetables, clothes and bedding, side by side.

I'd long to be taken out, wheeled down the road in my pram to the High Street and the jugular junction of Jubilee Clock, where the trolleybuses swung around and around, bells clanging, hordes of people shouting, market stalls overflowing, a sea of colour and vibrancy, the earliest of buzzes for a small boy.

And I'll never forget, of course, the other two occupants of 11 Springwell Avenue.

Tojo was a rather sullen sort of bright green parrot who spent his caged days on a wooden perch by the wireless set in the dining room, almost continuously crapping on the torn newspaper below. Just occasionally, he would interrupt his bowels to admire himself in a small spinning mirror and squawk loudly.

Granda said he was saying: "Who's a pretty boy, then?" So that must be right, and presumably that's what all the parrots say up Amazon Delta way, but it always sounded more like a squawk to me.

Tojo drank water, ate seeds and spud peelings and every night they put a hood over his cage like he was being sentenced to death by hanging. Which is ironic, really, seeing as he was named after Hideki Tojo, the ex-Japanese Prime Minister who ordered the attack on Pearl Harbor and was hanged in 1948 as a war criminal.

Hardly a role model, presumably even among parrots.

The second occupant was Her.

In the building's other rented rooms, at ground level below us, lived, appropriately enough, The Woman Downstairs. Never saw her, never talked about her, never even knew her name. But occasionally, just occasionally, there was... a sound. Or was there?

Somehow she managed to be the scariest woman ever.

And then, all of a sudden, we upped and moved to Hemel Hempstead. It was only 22 miles away in Hertfordshire, but effectively another world entirely.

"Be the making of the family. It's a godsend, a bleedin' godsend." That's what Granda said.

Granda knew everything in the whole world, although Mum thought he swore a bit too much.

15

*All dressed up in Roundwood Park
for the Queen's Coronation, June 1953.*

2
Chance Of A Lifetime

The New Towns Act of 1946 came into being solely for the likes of Mum and Dad. It designated eight areas within 50 miles of London to take 500,000 people out of the capital and enable rebuilding of communities blasted during The Blitz.

In the Harlesden/Willesden area alone, 1,300 homes had been destroyed and 6,500 damaged beyond habitation.

Hemel Hempstead was named as New Town No. 3, after Stevenage and Crawley and just before Harlow. After that came Welwyn Garden City, Hatfield, Basildon and Bracknell.

A couple of towns in Co. Durham – Newton Aycliffe and Peterlee – were also designated, along with Corby, Northants.

In each case, the government bought Green Belt land through compulsory purchase orders despite often furious local opposition. Cereal farmers in Hemel, for instance, were especially enraged to lose 6,000 acres of prime land, wrested from them in February 1947, a time of nationwide food shortages and, presumably, accompanying booming future profits.

London-based factories were given generous financial support to build new premises on specific industrial estates and their employees were to be given an allocation of cheap new rented housing aimed almost exclusively at young families.

To further fuel arguments, Hemel locals were not eligible for the new housing. Londoners only. That's how it was.

Instead of starting from scratch, the overall plan was to expand existing small towns hugely under the control of new Development Corporations rather than the established local councils.

The market town of Hemel (resolutely called Hempstead by the born-and-breds) was to grow from 20,000 to 60,000 in 20 years (now it's 96,000). The old town centre would remain largely intact, but be surrounded by neighbourhoods, a cosier word than estates, of up to 10,000 people, each with their own essential facilities.

To all intents and purposes, whether that was the planners' plan or not, each of those estates were to become small towns in their own right.

In Hemel, the first estate to be occupied was Adeyfield, the first families arriving in February 1950. Bennetts End followed and then Chaulden.

Little did we know Chaulden was to be our home for ever and ever.

In truth, there was little difference between them. Whichever segment you lived in in the new town of Hemel, a pub, a community hall, a church (of England), and an infant/junior school were within spitting distance of each other, along with a row of shops, which usually included a Co-op, confectioner, hairdresser, grocer, greengrocer, butcher, baker and newsagent/post office, each with accommodation above them.

As Granda said, the Act was a bleedin' godsend, although more accurately a much-needed initiative from Clement Attlee's new post-war Labour government.

Mum and Dad

Alfred John Riches was born on January 8, 1924, in Paddington Infirmary, Harrow Road, London W9 (from 1968 part of St Mary's Hospital, Paddington, but closed in 1986). He was the third of three children, after brother William and sister Lillian.

He loathed the Alfred bit, for some unknown reason, and I only ever heard him called John, although he always signed letters AJ Riches because that's what he'd been taught at school.

Ask about his childhood and everyone got the same response. He was scarred for life, he said, because he was regularly beaten by nuns at the Catholic schools he attended until, aged 14, he went on to Willesden College of Technology in Dudden Hill Lane (now the College of NW London), handily situated on the other side of Roundwood Park, and the adjoining Willesden Cemetery, from Springwell Avenue.

He struggled in most subjects, he was first to admit, but was keen on arithmetic (particularly mental arithmetic) and metalwork and did well enough to get a job a year later as an apprentice lathe operator making aircraft parts at Rotax Ltd, by Willesden Junction Station.

It was where he spent the war. And for the rest of his life he felt guilty about it. Which is why he rarely mentioned it. Nor much else about his entire youth, for that matter, except he and his mates regularly used to swim in the Grand Union Canal at Little Venice, which was so polluted with sewage they used to put their fingers down their throats to make themselves sick before the three-mile walk home.

Joyce Winifred Stephen Bugden was born on August 13, 1926, at home in Wealdstone, Harrow, Middlesex. She had an elder brother, John, and was to have a younger sister, Brenda.

She was saddled with the Stephen moniker because in the mid-20s it was widely fashionable for parents to give first-born daughters each of their own Christian names as the child's middle names.

She lost count of how many times people insisted she'd got her own name wrong and really meant Stephanie. "Oh yes," she'd say. "Thanks for pointing it out. Silly me." The accompanying look was never less than withering.

Unlike her husband-to-be, Joyce was no struggler in the classroom. At Bridge Junior School (closed in 1966) near the local railway station, she was regularly fourth or fifth in her class of 40-47 and described as "a good leader, most helpful, has worked well".

At her senior school, Headstone Secondary (now Nower Hill High School), where she started in September 1938, she confessed to being a plodder until war took over.

War or not, in reality her 1930s education didn't matter one iota. Top of the class or bottom, she had no ambition other than to leave, get married and have children. Ditto millions of other girls of the time. Her parents never encouraged her to do otherwise because no one expected anything else from their daughters. That's how it was.

War for her meant Wales. In the autumn of 1939, with mass bombing of civilians (and up to four million deaths) fully expected by the government – even though they didn't tell anyone – she became part of Operation Pied Piper, one of 850,000 children whose parents agreed they be evacuated from London.

It wasn't compulsory and the take-up was far less than predicted when the exodus was secretly planned as early as spring 1938, by which time war was perceived as inevitable by all but the more optimistic career politicians.

The number was more than doubled nationwide by children fleeing to rural regions from other potential German targets, especially Liverpool, Portsmouth, Bristol and Coventry. And more than doubled again by safety-seeking adults, mainly the elderly, pregnant or disabled. Plus the rich.

Clutching only the permitted suitcase, gas mask, ID card, change of clothes and a snack for the journey, the young Joyce boarded a packed train at Paddington Station and headed for the wilds of Glamorgan with her younger sister, Brenda.

At the other end, they were lined up on a station platform to be assessed by the Welsh farming community, rather like African slaves being unloaded from ships and sold to the southern US cotton plantation owners of the 18th Century.

"I'll have that one" entered the wartime English language, as the local householders picked the healthiest-looking while the sickly ones or those with a sibling in tow were left until last.

Suitably selected, the Bugden girls lived on a small farm and attended a village school for nearly two years before their parents brought them back. They both hated every minute of it.

Their mother, later my Nanna, always said the Glamorgan people resented having Londoners in their midst and her daughters never made any effort to get in touch with them in later life. In fact, neither of them ever went back to Wales. To be fair, the Welsh family didn't want to stay in touch with her girls, either.

After the war, Joyce was a clerk in the local Post Office in Wealdstone when she fell into John's arms, or rather at his feet, after a pre-Christmas drinks party somewhere near Oxford Street in 1947. He happened to be on his way back to Harlesden from his own factory do when she stumbled on the pavement.

He gallantly scooped her up, dusted her down and the next thing he knew he had a wife on his hands.

He always blamed the dramatic change in his life on Booth's gin and orange squash.

They were married at 2.30pm on April 2, 1949, at Holy Trinity Church, Wealdstone High Street, half a mile from Mum's home and seven miles from Dad's. The Reverend AE Stewart did the honours.

The financial figures involved take some believing, but these are as written by the bride at the time (I have the original document)...

Mum's wedding wardrobe cost a total of £27 (£901 at 2018 prices), including £2.95 (£98) for the shoes, £1.10 (£36.70) for the headdress and £3.80 (£126.80) for underclothes. That doesn't include the dress, which was hired, but included top-to-toe going-away gear, like a grey coat £6.75 (£225.30), blue dress £3.75 (£125.20), hat £1.30 (£43.40), blouse and gloves £1 (£33.40) each, handbag £2.50 (£83.45) and nightdress £1.25 (£41.70).

Dad splashed out £26 for his suit (£868!), £2.25 (£75.10) for shoes, £2.75 (£91.80) for his shirt and tie and 25p (£8.35) on socks. His total bill was £31.25 (£1,043).

Bridesmaids' outfits and presents, for their respective sisters, were £7.75 (£252).

The church ceremony was £3.15 (£105), cars £6 (£200.20) and flowers £10 (£333.80). The reception, held in the church hall, cost £26.45 (£882.90) for the cold buffet, plus £8 (£267) for the hall hire and band and £6 (£200.20) for the cake.

Mum's wedding ring was £1.55 (£51.75). Dad never wore one. Blokes didn't wear jewellery, he said, especially if they worked a lathe and had every chance of getting a finger ripped off.

They stayed in a hotel in Wealdstone High Street, by the station, on their wedding night for £1.70 (£56.75), then went on honeymoon to a Bournemouth hotel which cost £15 (£500.70) for six nights, dinner, bed and breakfast. Train fares were £1.75 (£58.40).

All told, with other bits and pieces, they ran up a bill of £152 (£5,077). The father of the bride paid for it all, bar Dad's clothes and the honeymoon.

At the time, Dad was earning £3.75 (£125.20) a week and Mum about half that.

When they got back from Bournemouth, Mum moved into Springwell Avenue with her new in-laws, seeing as the newlyweds had nowhere else to go. Until...

Enthusiasm for the New Towns Act swiftly took hold and when Rotax counted themselves in, with Hemel their preferred option, Dad jumped at the chance to join the scripted London exodus.

By 1951, there was a waiting list of 10,000-plus men from London-based factories wanting a job and home in Hemel and, as the largely Irish workforce toiled to pile the bricks high in Herts, suddenly Dad had a vision of a new place of work, a new lease of life.

At the new Rotax (much later, 1971, to become Lucas Aerospace) development factory in Hemel, he was promised a job in the tool room... and, crucially, a house to go with it.

Signing the appropriate form was the single most important thing he ever did in his life.

"Can't wait to get shot of the lot of you. Just think of all the space we'll have here now." That's what Granda said.

Granda knew everything in the whole world, although the day we moved out must have been one of the worst of his life.

3
And We're Off

Mum and Dad could never have afforded their own rented rooms, let alone a place to match No. 26 Benchleys Road, a pristine, brand-new two-bedroomed home, the end of a four-house block within a road of 34 houses.

It had a small front garden, a 60ft back garden and came with a generous allotment directly behind it, one of dozens meticulously staked out and given rent-free to each newcomer within a ploughed field which stretched the length of the road and beyond.

An offshoot of the main thoroughfare of Northridge Way, Benchleys sat nicely at the entrance to the soon-to-be council (no one said Development Corporation) estate but for now the on-going building site of Chaulden, a smart new area for grateful urban refugees.

It was half a mile west of the 19th Century village of Boxmoor, a further mile or so from the old established town centre of Hemel Hempstead (given a Royal Charter in 1539) and three miles on the green double-decker London Transport No. 320 bus from Dad's new place of work at the beginning of the mushrooming Maylands Avenue Industrial Estate.

Centec, milling machine makers from Richmond, were first there and already open for business by 1950.

The southern border of Chaulden (the name means valley of chalk), a mere stroll from Benchleys, was marked by a parallel trio of the Grand Union Canal, the River Bulbourne and the London mainline railway, the towering embankment of which loomed over both. Beyond were the glorious Chiltern Hills, home to Sarratt, Chipperfield, Flaunden, Bovingdon and Chesham, fabulous farms and beautiful rolling countryside. England's green and pleasant land.

There was no smog, like that in London which had killed 4,000 people in five days as recently as 1952. Fertile fields and woods, lakes and parks were all around. The stuff of dreams for the likes of us, and the thousands and thousands of others who were to follow.

It was a dark green Bedford lorry, smelling of oil and leather in equal measures, which took us from Harlesden to Hemel in the February of 1954.

The dirty-dungarees-clad driver let me wear his pork-pie hat as I sat alongside Dad on the squeaky bench seat while Driver grasped the wooden steering wheel with his fingerless woolly gloves and took us to the Promised Land, via Watford.

When we pulled up in Benchleys Road, 27-year-old Mum promptly burst into tears.

Imagine this.

Her husband and small child sat with her in a lorry about to deposit us in a barely-made road. Behind us in the lorry was everything she had in the whole world. Which wasn't much.

And yet.

She had absolutely no idea where in that world she was or even what she was looking at.

Along with a few other potential London escapees, Dad had been given a day out to see the new Rotax factory site on a coach trip to Hemel from Willesden a few months earlier. There was time to see where they could possibly live, too.

He hadn't told Mum much about it, mainly because the house (unlike the factory, begun in 1952) didn't actually exist at that time. He vaguely remembered walking with the rest of the daytrippers around the hundreds of foundations somewhere within a huge muddy building site, but hadn't wanted to get her hopes up.

So he had no idea of his new family home, either. He had simply been given an allocation, take it or leave it. He'd taken it. That's how it was.

By now Mum was trying to recover from the shock of her young life by sobbing and shaking and waving her arms about as Dad calmly produced the front-door key from within the pocket of his only jacket.

I think she was very pleased.

The new factory didn't officially open until about a year later, so in the interim Dad had to go backwards and forwards on the train to Willesden every day, walking half a mile at each end. Since commuting hadn't ever involved the likes of him, he called it Going To Work.

Back home, he waded into more work, creating a back garden from what was only an upward sloping patch of mud interrupted by builders' rubble and overgrown indigenous shrubbery. It was like a bloody jungle down that one side, he always said, although in truth he loved it.

First job was the creation of a concrete path right up the middle to what would be the vegetable patch. No time to lose, spring was almost upon us. We had to grow our own grub. Get it done now or we'll lose the whole of this year.

He bought me a small fork and spade so I could 'help' with the landscaping as only a three-year-old can, while he toiled during every spare hour of daylight, always whistling as he went into action against nettles, brambles and the dreaded bindweed, giant chunks of chalk and huge sharp flints devilishly wrapped in thick brown clay.

I could rarely attach a specific tune to the whistling, although Secret Love (by Doris Day) was on the radio all the time, so I recognised that because Mum rarely turned it off. And the old soldiers' favourite, It's A Long Way To Tipperary, was certainly on his hit list and highly appropriate since Dad marched, rather than strolled, everywhere he went.

Not that anyone knew where Tipperary was, of course, let alone how far. Could be just up the road and make nonsense of the title.

The lawn had to be laid from scratch, a lorry arriving one day with what looked like small rolls of carpet. By then, the mud out back had been sieved to a fine tilth and Dad carefully unravelled every roll, positioning them as though they were indeed carpet. There wasn't any carpet inside our house, that's for sure. Or anyone else's, for that matter. Lino and rugs ruled the world.

The turf laid, I was encouraged to jump up and down to firm it in place and hopefully close the gaps, then helped squirt the whole lot with water from the new hosepipe he'd bought at the Chaulden Gardening Club, set up by a bloke called Bert in an empty garage up the road, one of six built to satisfy the needs of all of Benchleys.

The veg patch blossomed. Spuds (no one ever said potatoes) and salad stuff, runner beans and tomatoes. Parsnips, carrots, red onions, mint and peas. Shallots, too, for Dad's unbeatable pickled onions. A patch that was by summer to become a feast for the eyes, let alone the plate.

The front garden was for flowers only. There wasn't much room for anything else after he'd put down a small lawn, but Dad made sure everyone got a colourful welcome to No. 26, the dahlias and gladioli waving hello in the breeze, the snow-like alyssum smothering the ground beneath them and denying the would-be weeds any prominence.

A shame that such visual joy has long since gone because those who designed Hemel, and the rest of the New Towns, never realised even poor displaced people like us would one day have cars. And that one day those cars would need to be parked somewhere. Like in the front garden, as we were lucky enough to be able to call it. Now a hideous slab of concrete.

Ah, well.

Inside, it was non-stop painting and decorating. Nothing really needed doing, but Mum said all the white paint made it look like a public convenience and she wanted it her way. Fair enough. No arguing, no point.

So every night when he got home from work, had demolished his tea and it was too dark for the garden, Dad was otherwise hard at it slapping on the Dulux paint, pasting Crown floral wallpaper on the kitchen table and hanging it precisely where instructed.

To my certain knowledge, he never got to choose a colour scheme. Not that he cared about such things. Women's territory. Never bothered with that. As long as it's clean and looks nice.

I dipped Giddy in some distemper once and we both got into trouble after I'd wiped him on the flower-pattern curtains. Mum slapped the backs of my legs with her open hand like she did most days and threatened to take away my pink (the only pink thing I ever had, being a boy) comfort hanky by way of extreme punishment.

The fuss soon blew over, though. She knew I didn't mean any harm and anyway, bright yellow wooden giraffes can't really help themselves, can they?

It was a cosy place, apart from the upstairs of course. Everyone got washed in the kitchen sink (me by Mum as I sat in it), then outside of summer months got their thick pyjamas on in the relative warmth of downstairs, wrapping themselves in a dressing gown before venturing upwards with justified trepidation.

Ice on the inside of the windows in the bedrooms was a common companion and sometimes it was so cold in the bathroom I rinsed off the Gibbs toothpaste, which had been smeared onto my blue brush, because I was too cold to stand there cleaning my teeth. Even in my fluffy woolly slippers with smiling bears' faces on the front.

Thank the Lord, then, for my wonderful rubber hot water bottle, easily my favourite possession. It was filled incredibly hot for me from the whistling kettle, which somehow made a mockery of being repeatedly told to keep away from the coal fire in the front room for fear of varicose veins, chilblains and all manner of other heat-induced ailments which would surely result in an early death.

I snuggled that bottle every night under my sheet, blanket and eiderdown, squeezing my eyes tightly to make sure I drifted off before either of us got too cold.

And safe in the knowledge we were the only occupants of No. 26. There could be no one living below the front room, could there?

A New Arrival

The first time I watched a television set was at 3.45pm on Tuesday, November 23, 1954. The Ambassador model had a 12in screen above a speaker set in a wooden cabinet which was V-shaped to slot into the corner of the room.

Ironically, the fascinating flickering light was the BBC transmitting Watch With Mother, which didn't totally work for me since my mother was next door at the time, giving birth to my sister.

I was in Betty Scammell's house in Walton Road, Wealdstone, kept out of the way while new life began a few feet the other side of the wall in Nanna's place.

Best friend Betty was a fluffy-haired pinafored widow who seemed permanently covered in lavender talcum powder, kind enough to make me thickly-buttered sugar sandwiches before I waved goodbye to Andy Pandy (and Looby Loo and Teddy, of course), and was taken back to wave hello to Sally Ann.

Sally could have been born a mile from home in West Herts Hospital (since 1970 Hemel Hempstead Hospital), but Mum wasn't having any of that. Unlike me, this offspring had to be born in her own mum's house with the statutory starched and plump midwife in attendance and presumably loads of hot water, towels and a bottle of gin.

You could see her point. It was the very room in which Mum had been born more than 28 years earlier.

Dad stayed back in Hemel, 16 miles away by train from Harrow and Wealdstone Station, going to work as usual. As was usual.

Sally became yet another addition to the bulging brick walls of Benchleys Road and beyond, where there were kids everywhere. All Londoners, or at least newborns, other kids to play with in a safe outdoor environment. But never indoors. Us kids never played in anyone else's house. Just in case we made a mess.

The only exception was if your parents had to go somewhere and you needed to be given tea or it was getting dark. But you never went further than the kitchen and you never, ever entered any part of a house without taking your shoes off. It was virtually a hanging offence.

The adults, almost exclusively mums, regularly went in and out of other houses, but it was always popping in, never staying in. Off with the shoes, then a cup of tea, a fag and a chat, maybe a Crawford's Custard Cream or a digestive to dunk, certainly never a meal.

The short-term visitors were all aunties and uncles, even though they weren't. Nobody ever called anyone Mr or Mrs unless they were shopkeepers or teachers and us kids wouldn't dream of using just Christian names for older people. Disrespectful – and anything that was judged as such was a major crime.

If it rained, we played in the narrow tunnels between the linked houses which led to our back gardens, watching out as our building-site roads were churned into even muddier swamps. Or, more likely, we just got wet.

If it was cold, we put on another jumper. All the kids had two – you wore the best one underneath in case it got grubby. Get them the wrong way round and you got another smack.

We all had nice warm light brown duffle coats, but no one was allowed to wear them for playing. They were only if you went out with your mum. Up the shops or something.

No problem, we weren't much bothered what we wore. We weren't going anywhere special, after all. We hardly left the estate. No need, really. We had all we wanted.

Hemel town centre was another place entirely. We always said we were going to Hemel without really realising we were supposed to be living in it.

No. We were Chaulden estate people, that's what we were. We lived in our own world, we were neither part of a broader picture nor had any desire to be. We knew nothing else, us street urchins, us toe rags. That's how it was.

"Live among your own, son. If all's well in your world, all's well in the whole world." That's what Granda said.

Granda knew everything in that whole world, although he'd never lived on a muddy council estate.

4
Hello Infant School

My first day at Chaulden Mixed Infant School, little more than five minutes' walk away, was Monday, September 5, 1955. It didn't start well, to say the very least.

No sooner had Mum given me an embarrassing kiss goodbye at the school gates and then fished her hanky out of her green canvas shopping bag for some reason, like she'd suddenly got a runny nose, I very nearly yelled out LOUD. It was... it wasn't... it couldn't be... it was... The Woman Downstairs!

Except it wasn't, of course.

The teacher I was very soon to know as Miss Mostyn had a long grey coat buttoned up to the neck, heavy laced boots and a bright red scarf. She had short cropped hair of indeterminate colour and an air of authority bordering on the menacing.

All the ingredients I imagined would go towards creating Her.

I walked gingerly down the path to the playground where the teacher stood, her arms suddenly and unexpectedly out wide, heralding a warm welcome as she grinned at me and pointed towards a door.

Inside, another lady smiled kindly as only such ladies can and showed me the peg on which I could hang my brand-new navy gabardine mac and cap once she'd checked they had Master S Riches name tags sewn inside. Phew.

As soon as those infant school gates opened, so did a whole new world.

I already had friends like Phil, Steve, Robert, John and Barry. We were as close as brothers, saw each other every day. Everything about us was the same, we were living the same lives only with different parents.

But, blimey, all the other kids now surrounding us didn't live in Benchleys Road or even just round the corner in Northridge Way!

From our allocated chairs by our allocated desks in Room 5, Miss made us stand up in turn, say our names and the street where we lived. All these people I'd never seen from places I'd never even heard of, although some of them were as close as a couple of hundred yards from home, none more than half a mile or so.

All scrubbed up for the first school photo, aged five.

Chaulden Terrace, Cuttsfield Terrace, Jocketts Road, Lindlings, Hazledell Road, Pixies Hill Crescent, Cotesmore Road, Middle Hill, Rowcroft, Newlands Road, Shepherds Green, Honeycross Road, Lucks Hill and more. It was like discovering a new universe, not that I knew what one of those was.

We were all London-born, all 40 of us in my class. Same age, same background, same everything. Lots of our dads worked on the industrial estate at Rotax, others at similarly large factories like Addressograph-Multigraph.

And we all looked the same. Navy shorts or skirts, white socks and shirts, black plimsolls with elastic stretched across the foot arch so teachers didn't have to spend half their time doing up kids' shoelaces.

All the boys had balaclavas their mums had knitted and thrust into their pockets, to be worn when it was really cold – with the cap perched on top. All the girls had bright woolly hats and we all had mittens kept safe on elastic ingeniously housed inside the sleeves of our macs.

And none of those clothes actually fitted any of us. It was as though all the mums had got together and agreed every item should be at least two or three sizes too big. Don't worry, you'll grow into it eventually.

We eagerly joined in all the same things, all of us keen to take advantage of this brave new world that had opened up in front of us, somewhere else to express ourselves away from the streets and alleyways of our neighbourhood building site.

None of us had ever been to a nursery school for the simple reason there weren't any. But we were all knocking on five years of age and eager to get on with learning.

Arithmetic? Bring it on.

"Once two is two, two twos are four, three twos are six, four twos are eight... all together now, let's hear it loudly... five twos are 10, six twos are 12, seven twos are 14, eight twos are 16... nearly there, a bit louder... nine twos are 18, 10 twos are 20, 11 twos are 22... AND 12 TWOS ARE 24!"

Cue spontaneous clapping.

Day in, day out, table after table, a couple at a time, Miss Mostyn helping as they got more difficult, pointing at the numbers on the giant wall charts and virtually chanting on her own as we got all the way to 12 x 12 by the end of each week.

And always with nursery rhymes to chant in between the tables:

*"Baa Baa Black Sheep,
Have you any wool?
Yes, sir, yes, sir,
Three bags full.
One for the master,
One for the dame,
And one for the little boy
Who lives down the lane."*

Followed by:

"Once three is three, two threes are six, three threes are nine... come on, louder... four threes are 12, five threes are 15, six threes are 18, seven threes are 21, eight threes are 24... step it up... nine threes are 27, 10 threes are 30, 11 threes are 33... AND 12 THREES ARE 36. WELL DONE!"

Straight into this, perhaps:

*"Humpty Dumpty sat on the wall,
Humpty Dumpty had a great fall.
All the king's horses and all the king's men
Couldn't put Humpty together again."*

Cue more clapping from us excitable little children.
It was fun. And it worked.
A faultless educational combination.

Every single child looked forward to it and everyone knew all their times tables before leaving infant school. They would remember them for the rest of their lives.

We soon knew how to add up and take away, too, using the simple hundreds, tens and units model, a tried-and-tested framework for success:

```
    H T U
    2 6 5
+   1 3 5
=   4 0 0

    H T U
    2 6 5
-   1 3 5
=   1 3 0
```

31

Reading could scarcely be approached in the same way, but nevertheless it was also something to do mainly as a class rather than individuals.

The Janet and John adventure books (based on the Alice and Jerry books in the US) were the key to learning our language in written form, our progression clearly marked as we moved through the series book by book, every day being encouraged by reading aloud the simple picture-led text, Miss Mostyn pointing to someone to read the next sentence or two and helping with any hesitation so no one lost confidence.

We willingly, if slowly, ploughed our way through the five books: Out And About, Off To Play, I Know A Story, Once Upon A Time, and Snow-White And Red-Rose.

The classroom was a cosy, friendly place, the walls all red and blue gloss, the curtains thick and reassuring, the big coke stove in the corner always warm and welcoming. No touching, mind, you'll be badly burnt. No one ever was.

There were posters everywhere, mainly of lions and tigers, cats and dogs, but also of the alphabet and those arithmetic tables, plus rules we were supposed to stick to, like The Toilet Must Always Be Clean, along with Put Your Hand Up If You Need The Toilet, plus Try To Use The Toilet Only At Playtime. And, probably, non-toilet instructions, too. But our reading wasn't up to those.

In the corner opposite the stove, the Wendy House loomed large. Named after the starring girl in the Peter Pan story, it was a plastic construction that looked like a dolls' house, but in which four girls could fit.

They used to take it in turns to squeeze through the front door and sit in there drinking their third of a pint bottle of milk every morning, issued according to Ministry of Education rules (Free School Milk Act, 1946). And every morning Miss used to tell them off for leaving soggy paper straws in there. Didn't make any difference.

Boys weren't allowed in it, not that any of us wanted to. It was pink.

For all the other distractions, the easel-supported giant blackboard was the focal point. On it, Miss chalked the letters of the alphabet, the words from the Janet and John books and all the tables.

She drew basic outlines of animals and cars, houses and trees, and we copied them as best we could on the large sheets of paper dished out every morning.

We were given Eagle pencils and coloured wax Crayola crayons to write and draw with, but we all looked longingly across the room at the sight of Kenneth, who sat all alone at a desk near the window, detached from the rest of us in our neat rows pointing towards teacher.

He had a lovely huge fat pencil that he grasped like it was a dagger and happily scrawled nonsense on his sheets of paper. We didn't have a clue what anything he attempted was supposed to be.

We didn't know he was a spastic with special needs, how would we? We just wanted big pencils, too, instead of our thin ones, but we weren't allowed so we all hated Kenneth. Really hated him. Everyone kept away from him at playtimes. That's how it was.

He even got a special part in the Nativity play as that nasty king, Herod. All the other boys wanted to be the king when all the parts of the play were explained to us. That or a lamb.

I was to be The Innkeeper. My only line, to be delivered when room-hunting Joseph came knocking on the upturned canteen table with a tea towel over his head, was: "What do you want?"

To which I added, in a moment of inspired ad-libbing, "...on a cold night like this?"

That was all from me, folks. I felt I was the star of the show and Mum agreed, so obviously I was. Neither of us could have known it was to be my first and only part in a play. Ever.

A lifetime's performance in less than a couple of minutes, guaranteed to make no noticeable impression on the rows of bored parents shuffling around on tiny wooden chairs pretending to be having the time of their lives.

The extra chairs for the hall came from the school canteen, the daily trip to which was pure adventure. Most kids hated school dinners (they were never called lunches), but I loved them. Yum, yum, yum.

Mince and onions was a magical combination, just the best thing ever, and you always got seconds because some fussy kids asked for only a little bit since they didn't like all the fat and gristle. Which was nearly all of it.

The dishes were all mouth-watering triumphs: beef cobbler complete with a scone like an ice hockey puck (I now know), rissoles (which have somehow become meatballs), juicy pork faggots with onion gravy the consistency of wallpaper paste, soggy cheese pie with a lone slice of tomato on top, oh-so-chewy mutton stew, sausage patties (the precursor of burgers), liver and tiny bits of bacon rind, meatloaf (could have been anything) and breaded squares of fish (Fridays only).

Too tasty for words and always served with boiled spuds or mash, a single vegetable – peas, carrots or cabbage – and a splash of thick gravy with lumps the size of rabbit droppings. Now there's a thought. We never got chips or roasts.

And the afters! Thick milky rice with a dollop of runny red jam you could stir around until it looked like a nosebleed. Rich treacle sponge pudding, thick crusty apple pie and lumpy snotty custard, tinned prunes in slimy syrup, frogspawn-like tapioca, spotted dick studded with raisins, jam roly-poly with extra jam if you asked nicely (of course we did). Food was never like that again.

Jugs of water on the table alongside two tall stacks of plastic beakers. Help yourself, blue for boys, pink for girls.

There was no menu, whatever that was. No choice at all. You had what was handed you when you queued up at the kitchen hatchway and made your way to your appointed trestle table. Everyone had the same seat for a year. You weren't allowed to sit anywhere else.

If there were any seconds available, a dinner lady shouted it out. No running, or you don't get any. You had to eat everything unless you had a note from your mum, excusing you greens or liver or something. I never had a note. No leaving the table until the plate was clean and your knife and fork were aligned together. No problem there, either.

The couple of kids who were left-handed regularly got their cutlery snatched from them and put in the 'correct' hands like they were in some way mentally defective. The dinner lady would then stand over them, watching them desperately trying to cut up a lump of meat while lacking all the necessary natural co-ordination.

If anyone was tempted to use fingers, they got seriously yelled at. That was completely banned, along with eating off our knives in case we sliced our tongue off. Fair enough, we could all see that. We weren't babies any more, after all – we were told that every single day.

All the dinner ladies were nice and a bit chubby. Dad said that's because they ate all the leftovers, you never saw a thin canteen worker or her husband. They all turned up for work with shopping bags, not handbags.

After dinner, we all filed out onto the playground. Rain or shine, that's where you headed, or at least you were directed. If it was torrential, they might let you back in, but by then you were soaked through so there wasn't much point. Morning and afternoon playtime as well, no one was allowed to stay inside.

Rain or not, we had great times out there on our large expanse of concrete. We were only allowed onto the grass surrounds in summer and then only if it was dry. Otherwise the groundsman would go potty, confided Miss Mostyn, who we just knew didn't like him much and not only because he stank like a compost heap and you could grow spuds under his fingernails.

He was especially unpleasant one hot summer day when we were all allowed on the grass to do some painting. He insisted that the very patch we were occupying needed urgent mowing. Miss gave him one of her killer looks and he did it the next day instead. It wasn't as if it was his own lawn, after all.

The concrete, though, was good enough for playing football and for cricket, the stumps chalked on the wall which went halfway round the playground. It was also brilliant when the ground was covered in snow or ice and we could make super-length slides.

There was the occasional casualty, of course, but any cuts and grazes were soon addressed by the duty playground teacher or dinner lady, who would spit on a hanky, wipe the wound and then smear it with iodine, which had the dual effect of burning like hell and turning your skin a shocking shade of yellow.

Mum took me to school for the first few weeks, then I went on my own. After all, it was just a few minutes up the road and no five-year-old boy ever wanted to be seen holding his mum's hand.

But every day, without fail, I had to wear clean underpants in case I got knocked over by a car. No one ever did.

"You get the finest education in the world in England. Every country's jealous of us." That's what Granda said.

Granda knew everything in the whole world, although his own school education was virtually non-existent.

5
On The Street Where You Live

When we weren't actually at infant school for those three formative years, we were in the street. We stayed there until our mums came out of their front doors and yelled for us to come in. Otherwise we'd have been out all night.

There was plenty of room and no danger. Benchleys had just the two cars as playtime obstructions and that was never a problem since they hardly moved from their kerbside resting places, apart from the obligatory Sunday afternoon drive into the unknown depths of the nearby countryside.

You knew when they were going out because they put on different hats and gloves and wore special coats which they called car coats. I asked Dad what that meant, but he just said they were coats people wore in cars, which wasn't really helpful. He didn't have a need for one.

The cars in question were both black Vauxhalls, one an old Velox, the other a new Cresta which even had a clock and a heater. They both had speedometers, too, so you could tell how fast they could go. Not that we had any comprehension of what 90mph meant. Pretty fast, but as fast as what? A plane? A train? Barry's dad's whippet?

Apparently, some cars even had radios in them so you could listen to music as you drove along. Right posh, we all agreed, none of us ever having been in a car of any sort, of course.

The owners had arrived in Hemel on a housing/job deal similar to us Rotax families, although they each worked at the Vauxhall car factory 11 miles away in Luton and still took the company bus which picked them up at the end of the road every morning.

Dad said they'd probably nicked the cars as they couldn't afford them on their wages. I thought they weren't very good at hiding them, then. Not in the middle of a road on an estate.

They didn't move much because Dad said they couldn't afford the petrol, they just had the cars to keep up with the Joneses, whatever that meant. He wasn't bothered. He much preferred the bus. More reliable, he said, and you didn't have to spend all Sunday morning washing and polishing the bus, did you?

The road was ideal for kicking plastic footballs up and down and for playing hockey with big fat sticks broken off from the allotment hedgerows. Sometimes we got a cricket bat out, but with one of those we were able to hit a tennis ball so far it meant more time was spent retrieving it from people's gardens at the other end of the road than actually batting or bowling.

It also provided an opportunity to enhance our cigarette card collections. All the boys had one, mainly cards that had been enclosed in pre-war packets and been handed down by grandfathers. Just about every tobacco firm employed artists and special studios and issued them in various sets, most often comprising 50 cards, before wartime paper shortages necessitated a halt. Later sets never recaptured that popularity.

I had a whole range, including film stars (like Gary Cooper and Greta Garbo) and footballers (Ted Drake, Stanley Matthews), British Empire flags (Brunei, Tonga) and military aircraft (Bristol Blenheim, Westland Lysander).

The rules of potential enhancement were simple. Standing in the road, you took your turn to lean a card longways up against the kerb – one of your spares, not one from a set, of course. The other boys would then take turns to flick one of their own cards at it. Whoever successfully knocked down the target card got to keep all the other failed attempts.

Marbles were acquired in similar fashion. A small circle was drawn with chalk and the players stood back about four feet or so. Taking it in turns, you tried to roll your marble so it stopped in the circle. No touching the chalk, mind, that's out. When someone managed to succeed, they collected all those that had missed. Sometimes dozens of them. We all had small buckets filled with the things.

We played those games in the road for hours while the girls played hopscotch on the pavements, leaping about over numbered square boxes, adding their scores together until they were out by touching a line, falling over, or both. Something like that, anyway. I had no real idea of the rules. A waste of time, really.

It meant all the pavements in the whole of Chaulden were covered in chalk. There was no shortage, after all, you could get a lump of it free from any front garden.

On or off the road, the only other obstacles to be overcome were the twin challenges of dog shit (squelchy brown in winter, a marginally less offensive crumbly white in summer) and tar-sticky telegraph poles, evidence of which was visible on every kid's socks and jumper.

When darkness fell, or bedtime loomed just as surely in summer, indoor excitement for me was provided largely by Dinky Toys, for which the front room rug was perfect. The pattern was multi-coloured squares linked by lines of varying thickness, a gift for a small boy playing on his own and focused on creating roads and parking places.

The Hillman Minx and Morris Oxford chalked up mile after mile, but the black London Taxi took pride of place in the make-believe garage (once a shoe box) in prime position near the coal scuttle because Granda bought it for me.

He'd even been in a real taxi a couple of times, in the middle of London. Piccadilly Circus, Marble Arch. How about that? When he first told me, I just couldn't wait to tell all the other kids, but no one believed me.

The new, much smaller Matchbox cars were very popular, too, but I always preferred the bigger ones. More realistic and less likely to get lost down a drain if you took them outside. I had lots and lots of them.

Along with stacks of used and therefore worthless bus and train tickets, I kept them all in the box on the back of the three-wheeled blue Raleigh bike Dad bought for me off a bloke round the corner who always had stains down his vest and a wife who was given to screaming her head off for no apparent reason.

Well, unless you count having two boys who liked to stand in the road pissing down the drains. She'd come out of her front door with a broom and smack the pair of them round the head, not that it bothered them much.

To be fair, we pissed everywhere – those two were just bad at it. Too rude. We all pissed in the allotments and in various bushes by pathways. Everyone was too busy to go to the toilet indoors. Unless you were a girl, of course, or you needed a poopoo.

No one did poopoos outdoors, not even the scabby kids of the shouty mum. But they did also spit a lot, which was revolting. Gobbing, they called it, seeing who could spit big lumps of thick dark yellow stuff the furthest along the road, marking their attempts with chalk.

There was no need. We all had hankies, which everyone called snot rags, tucked away in our shorts or up our sleeves. It wasn't the way to behave, toe rags like us or not.

We had our standards even when we got older and started a bit of pilfering and some petty vandalism. For now, the only law-breaking was confined to the occasional acquisition of a sweet or two, usually when the child was forced out shopping and while the mother was routinely rabbiting about nothing of any interest and consequently distracting the shopkeeper.

Sweets were big news. Wartime sweets and chocolate rationing ended on February 5, 1953, leading to a new centrepiece within small shops everywhere, like Mr Scott's round the corner in Northridge Way – rows and rows of big heavy screw-top glass jars encasing dreamy treats, most of them introduced over the following five years or so.

We all loved the likes of sherbet lemons, barley sugar, nougat, milk gums, liquorice shoelaces, rhubarb and custard, sugar mice, blackjacks, aniseed balls, peanut brittle, dolly mixtures, flying saucers, pink shrimps, fruit salad, chocolate tools, kola kubes and pineapple chunks, to mention but a few.

Everyone bought them in two-ounce (55g) portions scooped into a paper bag, a quarter pound if they were flush. Like never, in my case.

If you strayed from the colourful jar section, you could pick from the 45-degree tray-like display, neat rows of Spangles or Fry's Turkish Delight lined up among Parma Violets and Rowntree's Fruit Gums, Love Hearts and Murray Mints, Smarties and Rolos.

And there were the must-have Jamboree Bags, a lucky dip of the confectionary world. You bought them blind in their crisps-like packaging and might get some jelly babies or wine gums alongside a box of tiny crayons, a plastic hair slide, a mini colouring book, a yo-yo that didn't work or a cardboard plane destined to fly nowhere but into the ground as soon as you threw it.

It was boom time for ice-cream sellers, too, with seemingly every sort of shop (even our greengrocer) suddenly installing a fridge full of every child's favourite and more than 20,000 vans on the streets of Britain (there are about 850 now). How we longed to hear the Greensleeves chimes, a sure signal our Lyons Maid licking lifeline was on its way up the road.

We queued with our pennies at the side of the road for the crunchy cones or the more delicate and more expensive wafers, the strawberry, chocolate or vanilla ice-cream sliced on its wax-coated cardboard casing and slathered on the biscuit by the always-jolly driver.

On very special days you might get enough money for a Strawberry Mivvi instead, an ice-cream on a stick with a coating of frozen fruit juice that tasted delicious, if noticeably nothing like strawberries.

The only sweet things we were never allowed were chewing gum, because it would somehow stick all the bits of your stomach together and you'd die a terrible death, and gobstoppers, the certain path to choking.

Any cheating in this respect, Mum threatened, and she would cheerfully bang our heads together, give us a thick ear or maybe combine the two.

In reality, thankfully, there was more chance of finding someone whose arm had been broken by a swan than a small child with a dented head or a hideously enlarged ear as a result of parental wrath.

If we did get a medical problem, Dr Woodthorpe was there, in the majestic white house which heralded the beginning of St John's Road and the end of our estate, so big it formed the gateway to Boxmoor and the town centre beyond.

A man who seemed wider than he was tall, he swivelled in his brown leather chair in his front-room surgery, his tufty grey eyebrows hanging over the rims of his thick glasses, fiddling with his waistcoat pockets as he listened to whatever ill luck had befallen us.

He actually missed out on the only serious issue I had as a kid, because the nails of my big toes were taken out at Great Ormond Street Hospital in central London long before we moved to Hemel and I was still a toddler.

They'd apparently been growing downwards at a slight angle, rather than straight along like normal, which meant I screamed for hours on end without giving any clues as to why and being too small to tell anyone.

It was Nanny who eventually worked it out and when the more medically-qualified agreed and I was suitably operated on, the roots permanently removed, it was Granda who was most relieved.

He said he was glad there was something properly wrong, rather than me just being a pain in the arse child.

Dr Woodthorpe assured me I wasn't a freak just because all the other kids bar me had big toenails. He patted me a lot and said it wouldn't make a big difference to my life. Just one of those unfortunate things you have to accept.

I hadn't really noticed, to be honest. It was never a big deal. But for a few weeks afterwards I stared at any bare foot which came my way and made sure I didn't take my socks off unless I really had to.

He also spotted I had a lazy eye, so I had to wear a patch on the right lens of a pair of National Health Service glasses and endure the 'four eyes' jibes from those better able to see where they were going.

Somehow the glasses looked worse on me because my face was covered in freckles. I didn't like them much, but Granda often said they were worth a pound each, so that was all right.

I wore the glasses for a couple of years, I think, until I was about seven. I presume my eye was by then deemed not to be lazy at all, although I never understood what that meant in the first place and it seemed exactly the same to me.

Other than that, I just got the accepted childhood complaints of measles, scarlet fever, chicken pox, German measles and such – and a nasty bout of bronchitis which led on to pneumonia and a couple of days in West Herts Hospital, frightening the life out of Mum, who brought me sandwiches because she said all the food there was dangerous.

I missed out on mumps, although everyone else I knew seemed to have got it. It wasn't for a lack of trying – I was sent to play with any kids who showed the slightest symptoms in the hope that I would be infected and therefore avoid developing it as an adult.

It could be nasty, especially for boys, I was told by people who frowned a lot while discussing it. But never why. You wouldn't understand. Wait until you're older.

Things like styes on eyelids, corns and warts on fingers, verrucas on feet and the occasional boil on the bum were so commonplace, no mums ever troubled the doctors. Just bought ointments from the chemist in the hope they'd go away all by themselves after a few dabs of encouragement. Which they always did, of course.

Polio was the biggest worry for every parent, though. There were 8,000 cases in the UK every year in the early 1950s, hundreds died and many more were paralysed in some way. Mum and Dad both knew of parents whose children had suffered.

Immunisation was introduced in 1956 and had an immediate positive effect, but all us kids still hated having the injections. We understood well enough the need, but that didn't stop them hurting.

We had to go to the Lockers Park Clinic, opposite St John's Church, Boxmoor, and join a queue of others all standing there with their sleeves rolled up pretending they weren't scared stiff.

Oh yes, we were.

"Health is everything. No matter how much money you've got, it isn't worth a light if you're ill." That's what Granda said.

Granda knew everything in the whole world, although he was always suspicious of doctors and never went to see one.

6
Moving On

Because of sister Sally's arrival, the Development Corporation was apparently obliged to re-house us when a suitable larger property became available. It could take a long while and it could be on any one of the other estates.

Winner! In our case, the move turned out to be just up the road and meant much more joy for us migrants.

The new three-bedroomed house, 11 Long Chaulden, was only a couple of hundred yards away from Benchleys, first lamp-post on the left up the steepish hill near the start of Hemel's longest road, and even nearer to school.

It was fantastic, a terraced mansion and still within shouting distance of everything and everybody that had come to mean home on the Chaulden estate.

Upstairs, a big bedroom for Mum and Dad away from the road at the back, another big one at the back for Sally and a little tiny one at the front for me. It was explained I got the little one because girls needed more space when they got older because of furniture and make-up and clothes for going out. No, me neither. Never did get it.

Anyway, I loved my room, little or not, and the smaller window meant I got less ice on the inside.

We even got a new General Electric two-bar fire on the landing, which was switched on about 15 minutes before we went up to bed, always making sure all the doors were open to suck in the heat – although there didn't seem to me to be very much of it to suck.

There was also a toilet/bathroom and an airing cupboard with an immersion heater, which somehow excited Mum no end. Nice warm towels and no more clothes drying all round the house, she reckoned. Though not for long.

Downstairs was a kitchen which could take a table and four chairs, a larder with a concrete slab and wooden shelving, a large living room looking out on a 90ft garden and space under the stairs for hats and coats and shoes, shopping bags and miscellaneous other junk, of which there was no shortage in a family of four.

It even had a downstairs toilet just outside the kitchen, by the dustbin and coal bunker and the indoor shed which led to the garden. But Mum never used it because she was too embarrassed about her bottom noises. It didn't seem to bother Dad, who made lots of bottom noises. Mum said she was surprised the neighbours didn't bang on the wall when he was in there.

But best of all for Mum, the kitchen was at the front, with the pavement and its non-stop free theatre just a few feet away beyond the tiny lawn and cotoneaster hedgerow.

Sister Sally's arrival meant a family move to luxurious Long Chaulden.

Mum was a right nosy cow, Dad used to tell people. Though not her. Even as a little kid, I knew Dad was a bit scared of Mum. Or if not actually scared, not up for a shouting.

The kitchen enabled her to peer out through the net curtains, while the outside world couldn't peer back. How amazing was that? From her ideal vantage point, she smoked endless Weights, often lighting one from the other as though engaged in some bizarre economical project to save on Swan Vestas matches.

The radio was always on in the background as she focused on her own world outside. Housewives' Choice, most often fronted by George

Elrick, was a treat never to be missed. Music While You Work, as played in factories nationwide in a futile attempt to relieve mass boredom, was on twice a day, an expensive production complete with live orchestras and brass bands in the BBC Light Programme studio.

Then there was her favourite, Woman's Hour, with vital tips on using leftovers from mealtimes, avoiding dropped stitches, squeezing blackheads and burping babies.

And, of course, Listen With Mother, with indisputably the most famous question and anticipated answer of them all: "Are you sitting comfortably? Then I'll Begin." Never scripted, it was originally an ad lib by presenter Julia Lang in 1950.

The whole show was a mere 15 minutes of fairy tales, nursery rhymes and simple songs – nothing more complicated than Polly Put The Kettle On – every day. It drove us kids mad, almost from the moment we got past five years old, the target audience. But it didn't stop Mum, not for years, nor put her off the real goings-on in our bit of Chaulden the other side of those curtains.

She knew what time the woman over the road usually got off the bus on a Wednesday evening and would tell us how many bags of shopping she had this time and have a guess what was in them. "Wonder she can carry that lot. They eat loads of tinned stuff. Peas, mainly."

How the bloke at No. 7 had gone up the pub when it opened at 11am, even though it was the day before payday; he was a night worker and should have been asleep. "And he was there on a Monday, the week before last."

He was therefore either thieving or else keeping his wife short of housekeeping money – the domestic oversight being the more serious. Obviously, no question. No one on the estate could afford the pub on a weekday dinnertime in the 1950s.

"She's had that same flowery dress on now for three days," we'd hear of some other marmalised mum, most likely the Brassy Blonde, presumably named after her deep interest in polishing ornaments. She was also rumoured to be someone's "bit of fluff", a description which passed me by, even with the additional information of her being "a bit of a one".

And then there was the bloke from round the corner, who always inspired the knowing nod "he's never got married, you know". He was, apparently, "a bit funny" though we didn't have a clue what Mum meant, guessing incorrectly that it was because he had a beard when no one else did. That's how it was.

As a bonus, she could also spot the gypsies coming down the road as they so often did, banging on every front door in the forlorn hope that someone had carelessly run out of pegs or was suddenly desperate for a bunch of lucky heather.

We had to lay on the floor under the sink, holding our breath as they peered through the window and then moved on, apparently after showering us with verbal curses. It was a big deal for Mum, who'd still be shaking when Dad got in from work and she'd recount the terror.

He couldn't care less. He felt more sorry for Heather, his mate's wife up the road. Everyone, but everyone, knew her as Lucky. Must drive her mental, he said.

More welcome was the totter, who came most weeks. The rag and bone man, some called him, a lovely old bloke who stood on his cart yelling "Iron" as he guided his horse, Bogs (after the 1940 Grand National winner Bogskar), round and round the town estates.

If you gave him any old junk, and there was plenty of it round our way, you got a goldfish in a jam jar, and Mum gave him things she knew he'd want but we no longer did – any bits of metal and rags – rather than put them in the dustbin.

We always put the fish on the sideboard in a small oblong tank with tap water and a couple of huge mud-washed stones from the garden and sprinkled horrible-tasting (I tried it) food flakes on the surface from a cardboard pot with a plastic lid. The fish never lasted more than a day or two, then we chucked them over the garden fence into next door's bushes.

The totter had a side line in knife sharpening, too. And every spring, he'd take Dad's lawnmower off to be sharpened ready for action. Dad always asked where he was taking it and always got the reply: "To the lawnmower sharpener."

We had lots of regular working visitors, but every boy's favourites were the strongmen.

Once a fortnight, two coal-dust encrusted blokes from the Thorne & Son merchants would turn up with a lorry load of fuel they'd shovelled on from the massive heaps in the goods yard at the local railway station sidings, then transferred into hundredweight (50kg) sacks at their depot in Boxmoor, behind the greengrocer's.

They'd pull up outside in their black peaked caps and heavy overalls, pull down the flaps on the side of the lorry, hoist the sacks onto their shoulders as though they were weightless small children, then effortlessly carry them down our steps into the shed and hurl the contents into the bunker.

As they folded the empty hessian sacks under their arms, I'd pick up any spillage, marvelling at how easily your hands turned black and promising myself to wash them before attempting any more balls-scratching, nose-picking or trying to get wax out of my ears.

No lesser heroes were the dustmen who came once a week, picking up our heavy metal dustbin with no more effort than a coalman would show. I'd follow the man up the steps as he shook it into the dustcart and he'd let me carry the lid back as he returned the empty base.

I loved Lofty Lavender, too. At 6ft 8ins he was the tallest man I'd ever seen. Ideal for a chimney sweep, said Dad, he hardly needed brushes. He had plenty of them, though.

He was the same colour as the coalmen, but always wiped his feet when he came into the living room, a thick leather carrying strap wrapped around his brass-handled brushes. He'd spread dust sheets all around the floor nearest the grate, then poke a short-handled brush up the chimney, quickly screwing more and longer attachments to the first as it headed skywards.

I'd race out into the back garden in time to see the brush emerging from the stack on the roof, Lofty twirling it round and round as though it was triumphantly waving at me, its job done. Lofty left all the soot he'd caught in a bag in the grate so Dad could put it on his roses. You got more blooms and fewer pests as a result.

When he left, Mum spent ages muttering and dusting the whole of the downstairs even though she'd had the door shut.

We also had a monthly visit from the Prudential Insurance man, but he was as boring as that sounds. He came in the early evening and always wore a jacket and tie. I had no idea what he was selling, but Mum gave me money to take out to him and he wrote it down in what looked like a diary and always tried to pat me on the head as I closed the door. I made sure he missed.

Although we'd moved up the hill, Benchleys remained the favourite play area with its safe flat-ish road, the rain-proof alleyways and the tree-ringed allotments. And because it was so close and my mates had stayed put.

All of a sudden, play was all about guns. Not war guns or gangster guns, but cowboy guns. The toy shops were full of them, apparently because of a sudden surge of Western films being shown at the cinema and similar programmes on the televisions, which more and more people were getting. Not us, of course.

For no obvious reason, my favourite was Wyatt Earp, both a lawman and a gambler who spent most of his waking hours shooting nasty people. An all-right geezer, then, who became even more of a hero when I found out, a fair few years later, that he was also a boxing referee. Indeed, he was in charge of the famous 1896 fight between world heavyweight champion Bob Fitzsimmons and Tom Sharkey (and accused of fixing the result, as it happens).

As Earp the gunman, I'd stroll up the middle of Benchleys wearing my cowboy hat with tassels round the wide rim, in its shadow the shiny grey waistcoat I'd been obliged to wear when I was the obligatory cute pageboy at some uncle's wedding. Below, my thick belt, gun and holster.

The holster was strapped tightly to my bare right thigh with a bit of garden twine which Mum said could cut off the blood supply to my leg. It didn't.

The weapon of choice was a Lone Star cap gun loaded from a roll of tape which housed small black explosive boils that were always getting stuck when I pulled the trigger to fire. Even when they did fire, the noise was no louder than an impromptu sneeze.

I usually had the outlaw kings Jesse James and his Gang in my sights, no matter which kids had adopted the roles this time. I was even prepared to take on any Redskins who might get in the way. Mainly Comanches or Apaches, with the odd Sioux or Cherokee emerging from the alleyway between Nos. 10 and 12, maybe.

The James boys were often equipped with spud guns, a messy and inaccurate, albeit potentially more realistic, alternative to caps. The pointed end of the gun was pushed into a spud and twisted, securing a piece of flesh which was then supposed to shoot out of the barrel through air pressure when fired and arrive between the eyes of an appropriate enemy.

It rarely happened and the gunslingers were just left with lots of holes in the spud they'd nicked from their mum's larder and were therefore destined for a slap.

When battle commenced, there was only one rule of engagement: you had to take your shots. If caught unawares and someone yelled Bang! or suchlike, you were obliged to roll around on the ground and eventually utter a dying breath. Running off was not an option.

Nor was real fighting. Everything was friendly, we had no enemies.

47

Nor did we have much fear. Huge trees were climbed, barbed-wire fences negotiated, fragile garage roofs scrambled over. We'd play catch with sharp flints and throw knives, smuggled out of our kitchens, into the ground as near as possible to a friend's feet by way of fun.

And we got our dads to make us carts. All you needed was the base of an old pram – and there was a ready supply of those, particularly dumped around the allotments. Plus a thick lump of wood as a seat, secured with rope.

Then away we'd go, racing two or three abreast down the nearest hill in the middle of the road, steering not an option. The brakes were your feet, at the expense of your shoes. As we were constantly being reminded.

One friend even liked to sit his terrier dog, Yappy, on his lap as we zoomed along, dreaming of a glamorous life like Stirling Moss, Jack Brabham or Mike Hawthorn and racing at tracks like the Aintree circuit or Monza.

There wasn't much chance of me taking my pet for a similar ride.

My one and only pet (unless you count the brief relationship with various goldfish) was the only other welcome addition to the Riches family. Slowcoach the tortoise – the name's all my own work – was bought from a smelly pet shop amid a row of buildings near Marlowes Railway Viaduct, blown up (on purpose) in 1960 as town centre development increased.

Dad drilled a hole in his shell, tied him to a concrete fence-post by a long stretch of wire and painted an S on his back in white gloss, presumably in case Slowcoach acquired some wire-cutters to make a burst for freedom and could be easily identified among the legions of other tortoises looking for an escape route to warmer climes along the A41 London Road.

In winter, Slowcoach came in from months of eating dandelions on the lawn and slept outside the toilet in a wooden box packed with straw. Well, for one winter he did. He rotted during the second and Dad poured his body out of the shell into a bit of greaseproof paper and stuck it in the dustbin.

I wasn't allowed to cry, he was only a tortoise.

"Death is what life is all about. You have to learn, son." That's what Granda said.

Granda knew everything in the whole world, although he was lucky. Parrots lived for years and years.

7
Home And Away Matches

Once we left Springwell Avenue, we went back to Harlesden four or five times a year, I guess.

Granda and Nanny visited Hemel about as often, arriving on Platform 3 at Hemel Hempstead & Boxmoor Station from Willesden Junction on a Saturday morning.

Dad would buy a platform ticket to meet them off the train and haul their unnecessarily plump and wheel-less brown leather suitcase down the steep station stairs, past (but never into) the couple of taxis outside.

Then it was up Fishery Road and over the humpback bridge by the Fishery Inn and the cupboard-sized Fishery Stores, left along the unmade stony road, as we called it (actually Moorland Road), into Northridge Way then right into Benchleys an exhausting 20 minutes later.

To herald their arrival, I'd have my newest clothes on and my entire upper body (it felt like) would be smeared in Brylcreem, applied while being warned in advance not to lean back on the settee and make a greasy mark like Mum said Real Uncle John did every time they came round. It was a bugger to get off, she said.

It didn't stop Granda rubbing my hair by way of a greeting and therefore ruining Mum's comb work. Nanny just smiled, as she always did, and plonked her black shopping bag under the stairs, where it would remain until they left next day.

She wasn't one to fling her arms around anyone. Maybe a peck on the cheek, no fuss. She might even have been more comfortable shaking hands.

Looking back, I don't think I really got to know her at all. No one did.

They always had a cup of tea and some broken McVitie's Digestive biscuits out of the battered old Huntley & Palmers Xmas Selection tin we had for years (shame to throw it out), then Dad and Granda were off and running as soon as a decent time had elapsed.

I was left with Mum, Nanny and Sally as the men headed firstly to the home of a bloke up the road who collected bets on horses. Apparently he phoned them through to an on-course bookmaker in the days before May 1961, when off-course betting shops were first licensed.

49

Dad's bet rarely varied from a Yankee, an 11-stake bet on four horses in different races linked by six doubles, four trebles and an accumulator. Like all gamblers, he only mentioned when he won, which was about twice. Not twice a year. Just twice. Ever.

Next stop, the walk to Hemel town centre and the weekly market. Dad always went there on Saturdays and came back with a bag full of goodies – his word for edible bargains like broken biscuits, over-ripe fruit and maybe meat not quite still at its best.

But the shopping had to be delayed because in between was the Waggon and Horses, a huge pub (demolished in 1989) near the Plough roundabout, the entrance to Hemel's main drag, Marlowes, which housed all the new shops.

Granda loves it in the Waggon, it's a treat for him, explained Dad, as though he didn't much care for it himself or needed some sort of endorsement from Mum, which was never going to be forthcoming.

I didn't ever go in that particular pub or even stand outside, but on the other side of the road was a regular interruption to a stroll along Marlowes – Quality House, the Co-op's three-storey flagship department store and the biggest in town by a long way. It sold everything under the sun and even had its own bank and lifts, it was that big. It's now a Primark.

Mum went in there a lot. She hardly ever bought anything, but it had free toilets on the first floor.

She always had a cup of tea and a fag by way of paying her toilet dues, she said, although I think she just wanted to sit down and have a fag because she couldn't go for long without one and it was really, really rude for women to be seen smoking in the street.

What's the difference, I thought? They all smoke everywhere else. No harm in that.

Dad and Granda were always back from their travels in time for us all to listen to the sports results, and confirm their losses on the horses and football pools, while Mum prepared tea and Nanny sat there blank-faced, her thoughts as always elsewhere.

It was Saturday, so that could only mean a builder's fry-up. Granda's favourite, explained Mum, who certainly had never asked him. But whatever it was made a change from his nightly bread and stew so he was never going to complain.

Into two frying pans went, at various stages, bacon, sausages, eggs, fried bread, mushroom stalks and tinned tomatoes. Served with bread and butter. Marvellous, Granda said, you can't beat proper grub. Every time.

There was a reasonable gap between that and supper, when little Sally and I got out the cards and I showed her how to play games like Snap, while they had a chat. Not for your ears, children. Not until you get older.

Then Mum served up the Rowntree's cocoa, bread and cheddar cheese. No one ever had any cheese other than cheddar. We tried Danish Blue once, but it was salty and soapy. Or shit, according to Granda, who never held back on his opinions about anything, ever. I loved him for that and much, much else of course.

Nanny (standing on the step!) and Granda come to stay in Benchleys Road, 1956.

On Sunday morning the men either sat about reading every single page (sport first) of The People newspaper or walking round the garden pointing at things and nodding a lot. But they did have two tasks to fulfil while the women prepared the dinner.

51

As he did every Sunday, home or away, Granda sharpened the carving knife. If you can't shave with it, it's not sharp enough, he reckoned, getting me to stroke it crossways with my thumb in case I was in any doubt he was falling down on the job. The rougher it felt, the sharper it was. I always wanted to try it longways, but he promised me it would end in tears.

Meanwhile, Dad was hard at it mixing that roast meat essential, Colman's mustard powder. He always wanted to mix it with vinegar, but Granda said you had to do it with cold water. So water it was. Except when he wasn't there.

I didn't like it either way, tasted much the same as bitter aloes, which one of our cousins had to put on her fingernails to stop her biting them. It didn't work.

Dad had an uncanny knack of knowing just how much mustard to make, never failing to point out to us that Colman's made their money by the unwanted mustard that was washed down the sink as a result of reckless mixing.

They weren't making any more money out of him, no way. It was dear enough in the first place.

And so to the pub, a haven for the nation's men of a 1950s Sunday while the women stayed home and prepared food. It could hardly be described as a contentious issue because no one, but no one, ever mentioned it. That's how it was.

That meant the Fishery Inn when we first moved, but from 1957 the newly-opened Tudor Rose, just up the road near our school. Not nearly as nice, but very much nearer.

A four-minute walk to be precise, so Granda and Dad put their loafers on at precisely 11.56am and headed up the hill while I got my head into The People sports pages, digesting all the words I could understand, every statistic, studying every picture.

As always, the promise on return was of a Babycham each for Mum and Nanny and tiny bottles of Britvic pineapple juice for Sally and me, along with seafood for supper as long as the straw-hatted bloke was in the pub to sell it.

The dinner menu offered no surprises.

Sunday never varied from a joint of beef held together with string, plastered with Cookeen lard even though it was covered in thick fat, and placed in a deep tray in the oven along with some chunks of King Edward spuds at precisely 12 noon.

At precisely 1.15pm, on went the pans of heavily-salted water in which to boil the veg prepared during the morning – always carrots and one of cabbage or cauliflower, never both. Then Mum made a huge pot of gravy out of Bisto powder, which lived in a blue and white canister she regularly topped up from a packet.

When the men returned, at precisely 2.15pm with the pub now shut, the blackened much-shrivelled beef was plonked on a large wooden board on the table so Dad could carve while the vegetables were drained in the colander, spooned onto the best white plates and drowned in gravy, presumably in case they weren't quite soft enough.

Granda busied himself pouring the promised Babychams and pineapple juice, plus a pint bottle of Whitbread brown ale for himself and one of pale ale for Dad.

As the wireless on the windowsill spewed out the Billy Cotton Band Show, or a similarly depressing programme, as an appetiser, the thick beef slices were gently placed alongside the veg (never the other way round), soon to be lost from view as the gravy gently lapped over the charred flesh.

Before we ate, Granda always used one prong of his fork to clean his fingernails. Mum didn't like that much, you could tell. But she never said. At least he wiped the results down his trousers, not the tablecloth, and was helpful when we asked why there were always black bits in the potatoes. They were eyes so they could see their way to the plate, explained Granda.

After the beef, we had tinned fruit and jelly, usually Rowntree's lime jelly, which came in cubes that had been dissolved in boiling water and left in a bowl overnight to solidify into a tasteless blob.

Granda liked his almost floating in Carnation Condensed Milk, while everyone else had a spoonful from a small pot of single cream left on the doorstep by the Express Dairy milkman every Saturday morning, along with our daily two pints of silver-topped milk in glass bottles.

All adults slept on Sunday afternoons. It was like the law of the land. Spark out they were, Granda and Dad first, then the ladies once they'd finished the washing-up.

When they woke we had whelks and winkles, picked out from their shells with a pin, and brown shrimps, all from the straw-hatted bloke with a tray of seafood who had indeed taken up temporary but regular residence at the end of the bar in the Tudor. All served with Hovis and butter. You had to have brown bread with seafood. Rules. But never with anything else, of course.

Even better, alongside it all was a bowl of beef dripping from the previous Sunday's joint. How I loved that, the wobbly juicy jelly smeared over nearly-burnt toast, the pure white fat sticking it in place and the whole lot smothered in salt and white pepper.

And then Granda and Nanny were on their way. As ever, Dad lugged the suitcase to the station, as ever commenting on how heavy it was for a one-night stay as opposed to the fortnight's holiday for which it had surely been packed.

At home it was back to the normal routine, the weekly pre-bed bath, kids first. Coal Tar Soap for the body, hair washed with Vosene shampoo. Don't run any more hot water, you've got more than enough. You'll get chilblains.

Mum and Dad had a bath afterwards, ladies first. When eventually she climbed out, he topped up her tepid water with whatever remained warm thanks to the immersion heater.

It was the only time during the week that Dad washed upstairs. Otherwise, he always took off his shirt and used the bowl in the kitchen sink, doing his face and tufty armpits before having a shave. He dried on the towel kept under the sink and never in his life used deodorant. It was just for poofs, whatever they were.

When we went to Harlesden, Mum would pull out of her bag the folded sheets of yesterday's Daily Mirror as the steam train chugged into Platform 4, so we could sit hopefully unmarked in our smartest clothes on the soot-smudged seats. Not that the newsprint was by any means a guaranteed cleaner alternative.

The carriages all had corridors with sliding doors to individual compartments seating eight. At the back and front, there were no-smoking carriages. They were always empty. Virtually everyone smoked and it was an accepted way of life even for the few who didn't. Mainly children.

We were on the train about 25 minutes before we walked from Willesden Junction up Station Road past the gloomy All Souls Church towards the Jubilee Clock in Harlesden High Street.

Then along Park Parade past Granda's favourite pub on the corner, the huge Royal Oak, where once his Crib Champ pint pewter mug dangled from a hook over the bar until he fell out with the landlord and by pure chance it went missing soon afterwards.

He would fill it with his favourite draught dark mild on the couple of nights a week he ventured out for an hour or two, always alone, never with Nanny. She didn't like going out, he would confide. Needed a bit of time to herself now and again. He understood.

We turned left into Springwell, just beyond which were the massed prefabricated houses in Harlesden Road, erected for the bombed-out as a short-term housing solution almost as soon as the war ended, and past the lodging houses with their signs:

No Blacks
No Irish
No Dogs

Vacancies for anyone else. No problem. Never mentioned.

Poverty and vandalism ruled, litter piled up everywhere, buildings were routinely smashed up, stripped of anything of any value, no matter how little.

Harlesden was, officially, one of the most deprived areas of all England – and there was no shortage of opposition for titles like that in the 50s and into the early 60s.

Once in our rented rooms, Sally and I always got out the compendium of games. We never went anywhere without it. Snakes and ladders, draughts, ludo, a pack of cards, tiddlywinks and more, all manner of joy in one box and ideal for kids of any age. Little ones like her, adults, too. Easily the best value for money toy ever.

It would have been worth buying just for the draughts, which we played for hours on end, even after the dozens and dozens of games it took before we realised that if you know what you're doing you can't lose if you take the first turn.

The paint box was another must, every kid had one. Tiny squares of solid dry paint lined up within a long tin box, awaiting activation by the application of water via a skinny little brush housed in a jam jar, to be smeared on any spare sheet of paper and the resultant works of art proudly called Our House, Mum, Tojo, or whatever. It was hard to tell. The finished works looked much the same if I'd had anything to do with it.

Otherwise, we loved doing the jigsaws which Nanny kept in their original boxes within a pillowcase in the freezing cold spare room. London landmarks were favourite, Tower Bridge, Houses of Parliament and St Paul's Cathedral.

Same old tactics, get those corner pieces in place, link them together with the edge pieces, then go for the brightest colours in the middle and finally fill in all the gaps.

When it was Nanny's turn to choose, she always opted for a countryside puzzle. Constable's Hay Wain, West Country Thatched Cottages, Scottish Grouse Moors, that sort of thing.

We never fully realised she'd seen hardly any countryside in her whole life. Unless, of course, she wasn't telling us.

She never really told us anything at all, remember, especially regarding her own childhood.

Apart from a couple of seaside trips (Southend and Ramsgate I think), Roundwood Park – the size of 25 football pitches – was as rural as it ever got for her, an inner city haven described as 'The Garden of Eden without the serpents' when it was opened in 1895 'dedicated for ever to the people'.

The park bandstand was her only live musical entertainment. The aviary, which opened in 1955, the year she retired from full-time work, gave her a rare chance to see wildlife, albeit caged cockatiels and canaries. The spectacular water fountain near the main gates was her idea of going out for a drink.

Apart from going to work and going shopping, Nanny went almost nowhere else.

Indoors, she cooked and washed, sewed, scrubbed, polished and ironed. Sometimes she sat silently and listened to the radio in between making endless cups of tea.

I never heard her complain about anything.

Unlike Hemel, where we did so all the time, us kids were never allowed to go out on our own in Harlesden. It wasn't safe, we were told, and not only because there were rather more than a couple of Vauxhalls to look out for.

The perceived threat on the streets nearby came on legs, not wheels.

Nanny constantly warned us against the Darkies, the Nig Nogs, the Coloureds, who she said were in the alleyways everywhere and might jump out on us with knives.

When we were out with her, going down towards the High Street and Woolworths, the Co-op or Meyers the vegetable shop, she clutched our hands tightly and we had to cross the street if any of them approached.

She said they had black skin because they came from a hot country. They'd been coming over here since 1948, starting with a boat full of them called the Empire Windrush. There'd been a picture of it in the paper, all of them laughing and singing and wearing very bright clothes.

She had no idea where they came from, neither did she care nor make any attempt to find out (Nanny: they were from the Caribbean and by 1970 there were half a million of them in London).

The Darkies were here to drive the buses and trains because so many of our men had died in the war, it said on the wireless. They'd also be helping with the re-construction programmes and their women would mainly be working in hospitals doing all the menial jobs.

They'd been specially invited to live over here by the British government. They'd fought alongside our boys in the war, like so many other Commonwealth troops. They'd even been given British citizenship.

More's the pity, she said.

She never, ever, looked one of them in the eye, let alone spoke.

That's how it was.

Nanny never seemed to speak to anyone. Whenever we went out on a Saturday afternoon, she never acknowledged other women in the street. It was like she had her own corridor to walk along within her own world.

She didn't even engage in conversation with the shopkeepers she saw week in week out, even as they cheerfully greeted her. And she totally ignored the regular stream of blokes selling hooky gear out of suitcases on the pavement, for all the entertaining patter they provided while their eyes scanned the road for the Old Bill.

I couldn't imagine anyone less like my mum.

Nor did anyone visit them in Springwell. Nor did they go to visit anyone else, for that matter.

She sometimes took us to Roundwood Park, but that was about it. I loved it there, tearing around the wide pathways, going as high as I could on the swings and, best of all, straddling the wooden benches which doubled as open-air carriages pulled by a miniature steam train on the magnificent model railway which chuffed along between brightly-coloured immaculate flowerbeds until its demise in 1998.

We only ever stayed for a Saturday night, which meant me sleeping on the shiny plastic sofa which folded down into the world's most uncomfortable bed. No wonder I was always first up in the morning.

Dad said Rip Van Winkle couldn't have slept on that thing. I'd never heard of anyone with a name as funny as Winkle, but I was sure that was true. No one else could.

It dominated a front room where heavy red curtains reached down to the floorboards and pictures of age-old soldiers adorned the dull grey walls. There was a sideboard along one wall on which sat a couple of huge candelabras without the anticipated candles and a large Chinese vase which Granda thought might be worth 'decent' money.

There was a Chinese rug, too, secured from a jumble sale in a church hall somewhere, a huge thing with fire-breathing dragons all over it which constantly slipped from one side of the floor to the other. Mum said we had to be especially careful in case it somehow tipped us into the coal fire and inevitably signalled the end of our young lives.

The whole place was gloomy, that's what it was. It didn't help that the overwhelming smell was that of all the potted geraniums dotted around the spare bedroom down the corridor. It was a constant reminder that there was no garden for us to escape to.

There was no toilet paper either, just scraps of newspaper piled high on a stool in the corner. You don't need much else after having a tomtit, Granda reckoned. Waste of money that other gear, never knowing his daughter-in-law always brought a toilet roll with her.

He loved the genuine cockney rhyming slang favourites and used them as a matter of course, never for effect. The stairs were always apples (and pears), the road was the frog (and toad) where you'd go for a ball (and chalk, walk), his braces the Ascots (races), his hair his Barnet (fair), Greeks were bubbles (and squeaks), a look was a butcher's (hook), the eyes being minces (pies), his shirt was a Dicky (dirt) and his boots daisies (roots).

Us kids were dustbins (lids), routinely threatened with a kick up the Khyber (Pass).

Once we'd downed the inevitable stew, Granda guzzling his while studying the Daily Herald spread out in front of him, we'd prompt him to tell us tales of the Olden Days, but he only ever talked about his life as a postman, routinely shutting out any possible reference to his youth or even earlier life.

It was as though he'd been born in 1919, aged 22. Had no family, no childhood, no schooling, no early teenage years. Did he have a secret, as we suspected of Nanny? We'll never know.

The chat over, on with the visit's undoubted highlight. For me, at least.

Bring on the dinner table football. Cheer on the three star teams of me, Dad and Granda. Scrape all the crumbs off on to the floor (don't worry, Nanny will clean up), then erect the goalposts at either end – one-inch long thin nails about two inches apart tapped in using the base of the brass table lamp, the one with no shade. No point putting one on, the bulb was missing too.

The only other equipment was a halfpenny for the ball and a penny piece each, as your player.

Then, using a match to propel the player, you took it in turns to try to hit the ball into the opposing goal, or else move into a defensive position to block and bide your time.

It remains the best football game ever invented, although we had to keep rescuing the coins from under the sideboard and brush the dust off on our sleeves.

From his caged perch, Tojo loomed large over the pitch, regularly shitting himself with excitement.

If only I could have played that back home. But Dad said Mum would have a fit if I banged nails into her new G Plan table. She didn't even like us playing blow football, propelling a wafer-light ball by blowing through a straw as your opponent blew himself stupid the other side to deny you, inevitably covering the entire area in spit and snot.

Granda didn't care, though. It was just a table, he said. He never cared much about any sort of possessions. He was comfortable as he was, he always said, there were a lot of people in the world far worse off than him and Nanny.

Funny, I never really felt as comfortable as he obviously did at Springwell. And on one visit I even heard a noise downstairs that could only be... The Woman Downstairs.

"Me and Nanny envy you, living out there in the country. We're going to move there soon, when I retire." That's what Granda said.

Granda knew everything in the whole world, although he wasn't anywhere near 65 yet, so it wouldn't really be soon.

8
On The Other Side

Toe rags were a bit thin on the ground in Wealdstone, a nobby part of Harrow according to Granda, who of course never went there in his life. Apart from the wedding.

That's where my other grandparents, a touch confusingly called Nanna and Grandad, lived so we had to go. They didn't come to see us much in Hemel, though Nanna would have come more often if she'd been able to shift his arse, she said.

Their house was in a quiet, tree-lined road, the end of a long terrace with a large front garden and a much longer one out back. It even had a name, not a number, although I knew it was 1 Walton Road. And it was theirs. Jesus. Just imagine, a free home. No going to the Rent Office every week.

Mayden they called it, a coming together of his surname, Bugden, and her maiden name, May. They even had a front-door bell and there weren't many of those about. You didn't have to knock or rattle the letterbox like the houses in Chaulden, but I wasn't allowed to keep ringing it because of using up the battery.

They preferred to say they lived in Middlesex, which their postal address confirmed, rather than be thought part of north-west London, which clearly they were. It irritated Dad, who was proud to be a Londoner. Salt of the earth they were, real people, do anything for you, looked after their own.

Since Grandad was always called Steve, he and Nanna called me Stephen, the only people who ever have, although Mum would use the longer version on occasions of what she deemed to be bad behaviour, a sure early warning that another smack was imminent.

Grandad was a wood-working machinist employed to make bits of interior fittings for luxury vehicles by the local family concern of Hearn's Coaches, whose workshops were tucked away behind Wealdstone town centre.

He called himself a master carpenter.

Nanna dusted and swept and polished at the HM Stationery Office just around the corner, Wealdstone's largest employer.

She called herself a cleaner.

Having stopped at Apsley, Kings Langley and Watford Junction, the train arrived at Harrow and Wealdstone Station, scene of the 1952 train crash in which 112 people were killed when three trains collided during the morning rush hour of October 8.

Grandad told me that so many times I could recite the details. I think I ended up grieving for the victims.

We walked out through the station's back entrance, turned right along Princes Drive, then left into Headstone Drive opposite Nanna's offices, where we were always reminded she started work at 6am and was responsible for only the top people's offices, not the rank-and-file workers. Heaven forbid.

I always envisaged those minions, beavering away at whatever you do in a stationery office while knee-deep in dust as their bosses looked on from their sparkling desks above polished floors.

We were never told that beneath those offices was the top-secret Station Z, a bomb-proof bunker that would become the nation's Air Ministry if the Whitehall HQ was ever taken out by the Russians in those anxious Cold War times. It was manned by the mysterious Insurance Company.

Five minutes later, always mid-afternoon on a Saturday, we'd turned left into Walton Road and were indoors. And within minutes the procession of nosy parkers began. The kitchen door at the back of the house was like a giant cat-flap, offering unrestricted and unlimited access to a procession of unappealing neighbours.

They all wanted a cup of tea and a Bourbon biscuit, they all wanted to gossip about other neighbours, and they all wanted to tell me how much I'd grown since last time they saw me. Like they were surprised I hadn't actually shrunk.

I didn't like any of them, particularly the revolting 'Uncle' Lionel, supplier of Grandad's football pools coupons and there to take money for today's bets on horses and greyhounds.

He was enormous, had greying skin like a rhino and sweated until he dripped, even when it was cold outside. He repeatedly coughed into his hanky and scratched his bum with fingers like saveloys.

Dad said there were so many warts on his face you couldn't put a domino dot between them. He always smelt like he'd trodden in dog shit and would always be sticking his fingers up his nose to pull out tufts of hair which he put in the nearest ashtray, shortly to be seared.

His toothless mate was no less revolting, a dwarf-like ginger-top with a bright red face covered in pus. And none of them ever took their shoes off, although even Mum thought it just as well in this case.

We had to stay quiet just before 5pm as the racing and football results loomed on the radio, always the best part of my trip. Grandad scribbled the scores down in the appropriate column of his Daily Sketch and then began comparing those results with the selections he'd made on his Littlewoods pools coupon. Like 90 per cent of punters, he opted for precisely the same numbered selections every week.

He'd given up doing Vernons pools because he said he wouldn't win as much money when he eventually achieved his weekly target of selecting eight drawn matches worth 24 points. He was sure he'd get £100,000 with Littlewoods and retire to the seaside. He wasn't sure exactly where they'd go when that day inevitably arrived. Only a matter of time.

Grandad never won anything at all. Not a penny in his life. He always tutted a lot then screwed up the coupon and dropped it into the wicker basket by his chair, nestling on top of the already-discarded racing betting slip.

Soon afterwards, I was sent back down Headstone Drive to where a man stood outside the newsagent's by the railway bridge, selling the Evening News classified edition with all the football results and reports.

It cost 5d, Grandad gave me 6d and would hold his hand out for the penny (now worth 8p) change when I got back, even if by then I was soaking wet and/or freezing cold.

Nanna wasn't tight like that. Anything but. One birthday, she took me down to Wealdstone High Street and we went into the Sopers department store. It was even more posh than Harrods she said, like I knew what that meant. A big store up West, she explained. That'll do it.

It was such a nice place they even had these thick bushy coconut mats with Welcome written on them so you could wipe your feet as you went in the door. All the people serving were very old but they still wore uniforms, like they were at school. They called Nanna Madam and one called me Young Sir. That was a first.

The rest just smiled sweetly and stood about with their hands behind their backs like they were hiding something or had been interrupted while playing rock, paper, scissors.

Lots of things were in glass cabinets. You could see them easily although you couldn't touch. I suppose that was in case any toe rags had strayed there rather than stuck to their normal haunts in places like Harlesden and Hemel.

Nanna bought me a Timex watch, a big silver one with a black leather strap, with money she'd saved out of her housekeeping allowance.

It was my very first watch and I loved it. Couldn't stop looking at it. You had to wind it up every day by twisting the little switch on the side backwards and forwards a few times. Not too much, or it would break.

I kept it on even when I was in bed. But only back at home.

Nanna told me not to wear it when Grandad was around in case he thought she was spending too much of his money. In that case, he'd cut her housekeeping and she was finding it hard to manage as it was.

Aged six, with Nanna and two-year-old Sally in Wealdstone.

For tea, Nanna would make sugar sandwiches and something that went with my favourite Smedley's tinned garden peas. Corned beef, perhaps, or maybe Plumrose Pork Luncheon Meat. Ox tongue for special occasions, birthdays mainly. Always with a big dollop of mashed spuds.

Whatever it was came with bread and Lurpak butter. Especially delicious smeared all over the breakfast kippers, a true treat as long as you didn't mind half choking on the bones. Sometimes there was smoked haddock instead, bright yellow and less tasty, but it came with a poached egg sitting on top so that was all right.

Either way, it was nothing but Lurpak alongside, because once they went to Denmark for a distant relative's wedding and stayed in the home of a kindly neighbour so they'd save on hotel bills.

But they had a terrible, terrible time because their hosts were rude and often spoke in Danish, Nanna explained. They were sick on the boat journey, they slept on a settee and couldn't go out when they got there because Grandad said everything was too dear and he wasn't paying silly money to a load of bloody foreigners.

But they liked the butter.

So now, every time Nanna had a slice of bread she was reminded of one of the most miserable weeks of her life. And if we were around we got told about it all over again. So many times.

They certainly never went anywhere else foreign, most summers settling for a week in Margate, along with Blackpool and Scarborough the most popular seaside resort in the country in the 1950s.

One year they went to Ramsgate, but only because Nanna thought it was the same place when she booked through the newspaper advert.

She thought it was funny that the instructions she got, posted to her after paying by Postal Order, said they had to get off at a different Kent station on the train from Victoria.

The following year, it was back to Margate, even though they'd had such a lovely time. They didn't like the change and missed the couple they met at the same spot on the beach every year, who came all the way from Bristol, but were still very nice. Such lovely voices, like they were in a choir.

They always stayed in whatever boarding house had a money-off deal, as long as it was close to the seafront, so Grandad didn't have to walk too far to a deckchair. There wasn't anything wrong with him, he just couldn't be bothered.

In fact, he didn't walk to the deckchair. Nanna always got one each for them from a huge pile all roped together by a bright blue hut and dragged them along the sand to where he stood impatiently, gazing out to sea, having reserved the very best spot for Nanna.

But, more importantly, waiting to take the ticket, check the price and ensure she'd paid for them out of the housekeeping and not gone anywhere near their savings.

"He's such a lazy tight git," said Dad. "But don't tell Mum I said that."

As if. And no need. She'd long since worked that one out.

Kids weren't allowed in the front room of 1 Walton Road, which of course meant peering round the door and maybe creeping in at every opportunity. Otherwise, chances are Sally and I wouldn't have been interested.

It was horrible, you wouldn't want to be in there for long. And indeed, I never, ever, saw anyone else go in there.

There was never any heating, although a large electric fire sat in the grate, its lead and plug tucked underneath perhaps to avoid any possible temptation to adversely affect Grandad's energy bill.

The room smelt of dust, its two armchairs and a small settee covered in white sheets like they were corpses. The curtains, always half-closed, maintained the air of mourning rather than embracing the morning air.

A large brown rug dominated the middle of the highly-polished wooden floor, a fancy lighting arrangement (a chandelier, I found out it was called) dangling above it. Two cabinets filled the far corners, each full of really foul fancy glasses and crockery with pictures of royal people, coats of arms, that sort of thing.

Within the drawers of the cabinets lay elaborate silver cutlery in neat racks lined with green baize, none of it ever to be used.

On the wall were paintings bought from various market stalls. Mountains and cars, rivers and film stars, no idea who or what. Brrr.

In the hallway outside, a new telephone perched on a newly-painted shelf. Harrow 4912 was written on a bit of paper across the front of the heavy black plastic base which featured the silver dialling ring and supported the phone itself in a cradle.

In all the times we visited, it never, ever rang. Nor did Nanna ever phone anybody.

A huge barometer hung alongside, a subject of much more interest for me. I often asked Grandad all about it, what all the hands and figures and dials meant, but he was always too busy to tell me, what with sitting in his chair all weekend doing nothing.

Never mind, next time I saw Granda he'd sit down and explain it all to me.

The kitchen was different, though, and that at least was down to Grandad's otherwise carefully reserved energy. He told everyone it was the first fitted kitchen in England.

We had no idea what that meant, obviously, and it did sound a little unlikely, but it was a bit unusual seeing cupboards hanging on the walls.

Mum liked it. A great use of otherwise wasted space. Dad said he'd pinched all the wood from work.

More excitingly, they had a Kenwood electric toaster plugged into the wall above the triangular plastic sink tidy. How brilliant was that! Put your slice of bread in a special slot and up it popped when it was ready.

Every time, the bread was either burnt or wasn't cooked enough, but it was the envy of all the neighbours, said Nanna. They'd all been round to see it, brought their own bread for their tea and rushed home before it got cold.

Dad wasn't impressed. Back home, you had to put slices of bread on the waist-high grill pan at the top of the oven, pull up a chair and stare into the void to watch it turn into toast just as surely as your forehead started down a similar road.

But that way you got your toast done properly, just as you liked it, Dad pointed out. And with that admittedly faultless assessment went any chance of us ever getting a toaster.

Grandad had a large shed/workshop adjoining the kitchen, an ironmonger's dream of bits of wood and metal, tools and glues, brackets and nails, sharing space with a couple of deckchairs, table tennis bats (endorsed by the world champion and household name Johnny Leach) and assorted gardening equipment.

All the latter was for Nanna, who did all the gardening. Which meant caring for a large lawn, a rose garden and a vegetable patch up the top near the detached garage that was rented out to a bloke up the road who had a Triumph motorbike and sidecar and a wife who was a bit naughty, Mum reckoned. She looked too old to be naughty, I always thought.

The rose garden was full of really old plants which needed replacing, Dad said, but Grandad thought they were all right for a few years yet. Well, he would. But Dad was envious of the well around which the vegetables grew.

Nanna would remove the lump of wood which covered it and lower a watering can into the depths using the ancient rope and handle under the well's pointed hood, then spray the precious liquid over all and sundry.

The water made 'his' vegetables taste that much better than Dad's, according to Grandad, who told him as much time and time again. Dad said nothing. No need.

We were not allowed to go within 10 feet of the well because we would obviously fall in and drown within seconds.

The lawn was OK for kicking a tennis ball around, the coal bunker an obvious target, but my major interest was the Anderson Shelter which sat by the garden gate. It was full of overspill products from Grandad's shed, but in 1940 had been a potential life-saver for his family.

The semi-circular zinc-coated corrugated iron shelters were incredibly strong when half buried in mud, with more shovelled on top.

They could sleep six people and were to be occupied the second anyone heard air raid warning sirens, although in reality most people stayed in bed and presumed their stiff upper lips would be similarly bomb-resistant.

More than three million were distributed by the government to those with gardens within perceived danger areas, free to those earning less than £5 a week (£250 in 2018). So just about everyone.

As well as the family documents, Nanna used to keep all her glassblowing equipment in there during the war, every day transferring it to the kitchen to make as many test tubes as she could manage to boost the nation's medical supplies.

She was intensely proud of her war work, one of the seven million women in Britain who played vital roles after the Minister of Labour, Ernest Bevin, made it compulsory in 1941, at first restricted to those aged 20-30, later expanded to 19-43. She said she never took a penny in payment.

Grandad's war contribution was split between fitting out Army vehicles from his coach-firm base and his evening duties with the Home Guard, which centred on fire marshalling in the event of air raids.

There was plenty to do. By the end of The Blitz, in June 1941, 337 high-explosive bombs and two parachute mines had been dropped in the Harrow area. Grandad told us he'd personally put out dozens of fires.

Helping Nanna with her watering, aged three.

These days he could see the Anderson from his favourite armchair, handily positioned right by the French windows, through which he could also watch Nanna while he rested from his week's carpentry.

He watched her steer their Qualcast Sixteen petrol mower round the lawn, then trim the edges with shears before tackling the weeds, clipping the hedges and tending the veg.

If she was out there and he wanted a cup of tea, Grandad would simply bang on the window. Nanna would come in immediately and make him a cup of Tetley in his favourite cup and saucer, always accompanied by a Tunnock's teacake wrapped in red and silver foil.

When he'd finished, he'd place the empty cup and the foil on the floor beside him so it was easy for Nanna to collect it next time she came indoors.

Nothing, but nothing, about those visits was anywhere near as bad as having to sleep with Grandad.

No matter how tired I was, I'd automatically wake the minute he came upstairs to join me. He put the bedside light on and stripped down to his long-sleeved vest and pants, then put one leg after another on the bed as he unleashed his socks from their suspenders.

Never have I seen anyone else wear those.

Suitably attired for a night's kip (he never slept, always kipped), he tucked himself under what must have been the world's heaviest tartan eiderdown and turned in my direction. I was then treated to the unwanted combination of fumes of tobacco and his nightly whisky and ginger wine before he snored all night long.

Morning was scarcely any better.

When Nanna had finished cleaning the front doorstep with Brasso (she did it every day of the year, although no one ever used the front door), she'd lay the fire with newspaper and wood which Grandad secured from work then bring us up cups of tea and a plate of dead flies biscuits, as everyone called the Garibaldi currant variety.

Grandad wouldn't let me get up any earlier in case Nanna would think I didn't like her tea and biscuits. It would upset her no end, he said. I thought I might quietly explain to Nanna exactly why I couldn't stay there another second, but didn't risk it. I'd wait until I was older.

So instead I stayed put while Grandad nullified his impatience by using a spent match to get the wax out of his ears and smearing it on the eiderdown. Then he'd produce his beloved St Bruno Flake in its distinctive square tin with rounded corners and proceed to light his pipe.

I was distracted only by the view of the top of the wardrobe – stacks of Van Heusen shirts in boxes, none of them ever opened. Which didn't stop Mum and Dad getting him another one every birthday and Christmas. They were his favourite, after all. Loved them.

He could have opened a bloody shop, said Dad, who didn't seem to like Grandad much and could have done with a few more shirts of his own.

I always felt guilty that I loved Granda more than Grandad, so I didn't tell anyone except Sally. I think she understood.

We never went out much in Wealdstone, because Dad always needed to get back for something early on the Sunday. The Tudor Rose, probably. Couldn't blame him. We all wanted to get back.

Once we were staying there and it was very hot and we could have gone to Wealdstone Open Air Swimming Baths, right near the station and so handy for the train home.

But Mum wouldn't go there. She never wore a swimming costume. Too thin, she said. People would be diving in from all round the pool, desperately trying to stop her getting sucked down the plughole.

She had a real thing about being too skinny and used to stir this special powdered stuff into warm milk in an attempt to put on weight. She bought lots and lots of boxes of it, but it didn't seem to make much difference and cost far too much.

I think being 5ft 10ins made her feel thinner, as though she was somehow being stretched skywards. The same weight on a 5ft 5in frame might have suited her better, Dad reckoned. I don't think he told her that, though.

Back home, when no visits in either direction were imminent, Mum made the five-minute walk to the phone box to call Nanna once a week, always a Friday evening.

She'd put her cream furry-collared coat on over her pink corduroy dressing gown and stuff an orange-and-green packet of five Woodbine (the Weights were long gone) in the pocket along with a handful of 1d coins. If it was wet, she'd put shiny shoes on instead of her pointy pink zip-up slippers. But only if.

She took me once to show me how the phone worked, dialling HAR4912 and putting four coins in the slot beneath the phone.

The phone the other end would ring a few times, then Nanna

answered and Mum pressed button A to begin her timed call. Never Grandad, who explained he never knew who was calling and they wouldn't want to talk to him anyway, so what was the point of getting up and walking all the way to the hall? May as well stay in his armchair after working hard all week.

All the time Mum was out phoning, Dad would look anxiously at the Metamec clock on the kitchen wall. There was no safety issue, he just knew he couldn't go to the Tudor Rose until she got back because of leaving us kids on our own.

Friday night was darts night with Ron and Fred. Never missed. Get your name on the scoreboard, take chalks, stay on till you get beat. A free pint from the guv'nor if you scored 180. It never happened.

Dad wore his usual – slacks, his favourite open-necked shirt he'd bought from the outfitters Cecil Gee, and maybe a cardigan, one of Mum's knitting triumphs since he wasn't allowed to wear anything else in that line. Ties, like his only suit, were for weddings, christenings and funerals. Literally, nothing else.

It was not as though he'd be going to a posh restaurant or a job interview. He never went to either.

As Mum approached the front door, he put on his favourite deck shoes and headed hillwards to the Tudor. The game was 301, start and finish on a double. Dad always tried to get off on 14s.

"Wealdstone's not my cup of tea. All those people there who think they own their own houses. They don't. They're debtors, son, bleedin' debtors, that's all. The bank owns the house. OK, we own nothing, but we don't owe nothing either." That's what Granda said.

Granda knew everything in the whole world, although it annoyed Mum that he didn't have any respect for where she came from.

9

Holidays

We didn't go on holiday much. And when we did, the actual dates weren't a problem.

Like all the factories in Hemel, Rotax shut down completely for two weeks every year. There was an annual democratic vote to decide precisely when, but because all the men had kids it had to be during the six-week school summer holidays.

Other holidays were just Bank Holiday days off. Two weeks was your lot.

Some of the men didn't even want two weeks off, since those on the shop floor (like Dad) didn't get paid. No money coming in, the same bills to pay, and expected to take your family on holiday in August, even in those days the most expensive time to do so.

Anyway, on with Mum's matching comfy jumpers, an easy way of telling the world We're On Holiday, presumably because you wouldn't be seen dead in them otherwise. Identical little and large versions for sons and dads (blue-based), ditto for daughters and mums (pinkish).

All families did it, the jumpers knitted during the winter months and no one allowed to wear them until it was (hopefully) warm and sunny in August. Then those jumpers became the following winter jumpers, and so on and so on.

For most mums of the time, knitting was second only to ironing and just ahead of sewing, darning and polishing ugly brass ornaments on their list of wonderful ways to spend an evening, so at least that dedication was showcased annually.

Two holidays stand out because they were the only times we had a whole week away in our jumpers. And the obligatory white ankle socks and new sandals, of course.

The Isle of Wight boarding house in Ryde smelt strongly of bleach and was run by a cube-shaped woman who looked like a boxer dog, her face permanently scrunched as if someone was standing on her toes. If there was a man on the scene, he kept so well hidden we didn't see him all week. Hard to blame him.

We were the only people staying there, although she reckoned she was always packed out. So we were very lucky. Most popular place in town. Been going years. Lots of famous people had stayed, but she didn't like to name names, you know. Discreet.

We shared a big room with one big bed and two little ones and there was a toilet and bathroom down a long corridor. If we wanted to have a bath, we had to pay extra, so we just washed in the sink in the corner with the water from a huge jug and a bar of soap wrapped in waxy paper.

She made us a nice breakfast, starting with porridge and asking us if we wanted sugar or salt on it. Salt. Ho ho. Couldn't wait to tell our mates. Yes, salt. Pull the other leg.

After that, we got eggs (poached or fried) on toast and we could have as many cups of tea as we liked. We got the same every day. Dad said he was surprised he hadn't read about the shortage of bacon and sausages on the island.

Then she kicked us out at 10am and most days we got the Southern Vectis bus for a 20-minute ride to Cowes then walked for about half an hour to Gurnard Bay, past the golf course. The beach was better there, said Dad, even though it was all pebbles. Every day, Mum asked why we weren't staying there, then.

On the way, she bought a loaf of bread, which the baker sliced in his special machine, a small pack of butter and some luncheon meat, and made us sandwiches. Sometimes we had a Bowyers pork pie and Smith's crisps as well, the packets with the twisted tiny blue bags of salt in them.

Or not, there was no guarantee. Sometimes you didn't get one at all, another time you got four or five. Mum would keep any extras in her handbag in case we were unlucky next time.

We ate them with Mum, sitting on a wall by some flowerbeds while Dad went in the Woodvale pub for his pint at lunchtime. Just the one, mind, don't be long.

When it rained, we put on our plastic Pakamacs ('The Raincoat In Your Pocket'), stayed on the bus and went round and round the island. Apparently, you just bought this one family ticket which lasted a week and you could go on as many bus rides as you liked. Mum said they should do that in Hemel, but she wasn't holding her breath.

Once, when the sun came out, we stopped off in Sandown where they had a funfair that included driving little electric boats round a kind of water-filled racetrack. You could stay on as long as you wanted because there were hardly any kids there. How good was that! Easily the highlight of the whole holiday.

We weren't allowed back in the B&B until five, even on days when it was chucking it down. And "under no circumstances" were we to bring any food back in with us, especially fish and chips. "They stink the place out." She was sure we'd understand.

So we ate them, every day, squeezed onto a wooden bench opposite the Boxer's grey-bricked terraced house, finishing them at 5.01 even though we got our evening meal at 6pm sharp. Those fish and chips were brilliant, straight out of the boat and into the fryer, said Dad. You'll never taste the likes of them again.

Which was considerably more than could be said for Boxer's culinary expertise, which started and finished with meanly-packed pies of dubious origin, mash and gravy. Every night.

It would have made a great picture, that bench. Not that we ever owned a camera, of course.

After tea, we played ludo or other board games at the table until bedtime and after a week we weren't too disappointed to be heading home from Ryde Pier to Portsmouth Harbour Station on a packed paddle steamer called the Whippingham, destined to be scrapped in 1963.

One of the crew members proudly told us how the ship had been used during the heroic evacuation of Dunkirk in May 1940. It had no weapons of its own, yet had reached the beaches under heavy fire, rescuing hundreds of troops who would otherwise have been killed or at least taken prisoner by the Germans.

The troops must have had more room than we did, said Dad, astride the suitcases.

Next stop Waterloo Station courtesy of Southern Railways, then across London by Tube to Euston and eventually home after what seemed an age. Particularly for Dad with all our gear. Like a bloody packhorse.

Much more friendly times were had at the Constitutional Holiday Camp at Hopton-on-Sea, established by a far-seeing Norfolk businessman as early as 1933. Based on traditional Army camp designs, it had been transformed into comparative leisurely luxury by the late 1950s (now re-born as a Haven Holiday Village).

I loved it there, we all did.

Home from home was a very modest chalet, a nice word which in reality meant small concrete box. There were at least 60 of them enclosing a large rectangular playing field, rather like Wild West-bound American settlers' wagons fearful of an uninvited visit from marauding

Red Indians only a century or so earlier.

Each Hopton home boasted four one-size camp beds, a large wardrobe with hooks but no hangers and a white porcelain wash basin and tap which sporadically spewed out lukewarm water. Just the job, we all agreed.

Toilets and showers were in a communal block across the field, but Dad said if we needed to go in the night we could just nip round the back – but whatever you do, watch where you're treading. You never know.

Which is what everyone in the camp did. He said it was like Oxford Circus about 3am.

I was nervous about the idea of using the showers because I'd never been in one in my life, but it didn't matter. I'd had a bath before we left Hemel and we were only there a week.

Mum was the only one who went over to the block every morning. Dad said she had to wash her bits in hot water. Our bits were clearly of less importance.

There were two scruffy grass tennis courts with nets of a similar standard, which were never used, and the centrepiece, the huge clubhouse, which provided all we needed.

Half of it was the canteen, which operated just like the one at school. You queued up with a tray, got your food dished out by a large smiling woman with a white, but somewhat stained, apron and sat at the same wooden seat at a huge long table all week, the seat numbers matching those of the chalets.

Everyone talked to everyone else and everyone came from places no one else had ever heard of, let alone been to. Absolutely no one had heard of Hemel Hempstead, so it was a waste of time mentioning Chaulden. It was fascinating. Some kids even talked so funny we could hardly understand what they were saying, but we all got on great.

All the girls swapped addresses and became pen friends so they could trace each other's lives and then meet up again in the distant future and go on exciting holidays together to other countries, like America. All before going to their weddings and being godmothers to their children.

Maximum time for a penfriend: two letters. The boys didn't bother.

The food was really lovely. Breakfast was Cornflakes or Weetabix, fried beef sausages or bacon and eggs with bread and butter. As much bread as you liked, and really crusty.

For tea, you always got a choice of two meat things. I can't remember any, they all looked much the same, but they were really nice and they did big fat chips. So we had chips every day, no matter what the accompaniment. And they had fruit puddings and let you have pink blancmange with it if you said you didn't like custard. So Sally and I pretended we didn't so we got that every day, too.

Mum had to buy grub for the afternoon from the Hopton Village Stores by the camp gates, because that wasn't included in what Dad had paid for the holiday. But they sold ready-made sandwiches, stacked up on the counter in a big plastic case by the newspapers.

We hadn't seen those before, so it was brilliant and more importantly no work for Mum while she was on her holidays, she said. Beef, cheese, any paste you liked and one day we even had chicken. Dad said the bread was always stale and there wasn't enough butter. Mum could have done much better for far cheaper.

I bought loads and loads of sweets in there, and frozen Jubbly orange drinks, with all the threepenny bits I'd saved up and kept under my pillow in an old tobacco tin. I went so often they knew my name, although they called me Stephen rather than Steve because it was on my holiday camp badge on my jumper, which made me a bit cross.

I was too shy to ask them to call me Steve.

The other part of the clubhouse was the Happy Hopton Hall, the fun up and running even as the canteen tables were being swabbed down with cloths that had seen better times.

The early evening entertainment was identical to the lunchtime entertainment. Bingo, played to packed houses, almost exclusively women who would elbow each other out of the way to get seats near the front, as though they were all as deaf as posts.

They went mental in there, Dad reckoned, who never went to bingo anywhere in his life and wasn't about to start now. Not the thing for real blokes. What next, those coffee mornings he'd heard about?

Even worse than whist drives, which they only played in old folks' homes that unfailingly stank to high heaven. They probably had those stupid beetle drives there, too, although he never explained exactly what they were either.

"All the fours 44, two fat ladies 88, three and five 35, unlucky for some 13, clickety-click 66..." Bloody stupid, he said.

At last, the bingo tables cleared, the bar raided for beers and gins when it opened at 7pm, on came the stars of the evening show. Always a comedian to start with, obliged to stay all night and perform the MC duties as well.

He'd introduce pianists and singers mostly, usually "interrupting their country-wide tour to be here with you lucky people tonight" and maybe a couple of magicians doing card tricks only the front row of seats had a snowball in hell's chance of being able to see. A bloke with an accordion once, who made the most appalling row.

Mum thought they were all great, they should be in the West End. Dad thought it stupid he couldn't get up and get another beer while the acts were on.

There was a gap during the evening so all us kids could be put to bed before the loud band music started and the mums and dads were invited to dance the night away. Well, not all of it. Only until 11pm, half an hour after the bar shut.

Most nights they were back before we were asleep, although we pretended to be.

During the day, there was no let-up in the action, most of it competitions organised by the staff of enthusiastic local teenagers wearing T-shirts with smiley faces on the front. Darts and snooker, cribbage and dominoes took their place alongside fancy dress, knobbly knees, limbo dancing, bathing beauties, loudest shout, most glamorous granny, prettiest baby and, oddest of all, The Man Who Could Keep His Pipe Alight Longest.

For kids, there were treasure hunts, drawing competitions and a week-long sports day with sack races, egg and spoon, skipping, high jump, long jump, throwing the cricket ball and various running races all ending up with Finals Day Friday.

I won the 100 yards and got a red table tennis bat with dimples and was really embarrassed when people started clapping when the prizes were given out in the hall after tea, just after I'd got brown sauce all down the shirt I was supposed to be wearing home next day.

We went to the lovely Hopton-on-Sea beach some days and once even got on the camp bus for the five-mile ride to Great Yarmouth, where I ate eels, cockles and whelks from a stall on the promenade with Dad.

The girls (he always called them that) went wandering around the shops without managing to buy anything at all, as usual, and we all met up at the funfair and went on the dodgems, holding the biggest candyflosses ever. Just brilliant.

Otherwise, summer holidays with Mum and Dad meant occasional days out and they were indeed few and far between.

Those matching jumpers lived to fight another day when we went to Windsor, not an easy place to get to from Hemel if you don't have a car. It meant a four-mile bus trip to Berkhamsted and a long wait by the railway station to get another bus the 25 miles to Windsor, by which time I'd eaten my packed lunch and felt really sick.

And lo and behold, I duly was during our special treat, a 40-minute boat trip from Windsor to Boveney Lock and back, treating the flowing waters of the Thames below to unwanted big chunks of Shippam's bloater paste sandwiches and lumps of thick greasy pastry that had once been home to some indigestible sausage meat.

When we got off the boat I had my picture taken with Sally because Mum wanted a souvenir and, handily placed there by the gangplank was none other than The Original Birdman, not to be confused with all those other birdmen, I thought. Not that there were any.

These horrible cockatoos (I think they were) were placed on our heads and we smiled sweetly to make Mum pleased while the Birdman pressed his camera button. Then we went back just before going home to get the finished prints.

We never went round Windsor Castle because the tickets were too expensive. But Dad bought a couple of postcards so we knew what the inside looked like and that was good enough for me. I still felt a bit sick.

Other day trips during the summer were always coach outings to the seaside – you could choose from Brighton, Littlehampton, Clacton, Bognor and Southend. Don't remember anywhere else.

We'd book tickets from the sweet shop up the road and clamber on a beaten-up old banger from Bream Coaches in the car park outside there at about 7am on a Sunday morning, the same families going all the time, all of us exclusively from Chaulden.

Despite the unearthly hour, Mum never let us out of the house without food. Never did, no matter what. We'd be fuelled by a breakfast courtesy of Kellogg's, with three or four teaspoons of added sugar from the pot.

We had different boxes of cereal every week, shamelessly influenced by whatever free gift was flagged up on the outside, to be found by rummaging around amid the boring dried fodder inside.

It could be a plastic submarine, a spinning top or even a Noddy transfer to stick on the back of your hand. All of them of minimal interest and very soon discarded. But free, that was the key.

We also got a slice of bread fried in dripping with either sugar or a fried egg on top (never both) and maybe some mushroom stalks, never the tops. I really wanted a boiled egg with soldiers, but I didn't like eating the white so Mum wouldn't let me. She'd never have any waste.

Ten months old and making waves on a day trip to Bognor with Aunty Brenda (left) and Mum.

It was always dark when we got home from the seaside because we had to stop at a pub on the way back. The kids either stayed on the coach, lots of them going to sleep, or stood in the car park getting drinks and crisps sent out. I went for the cream soda option.

Then we all had to stop again later on by the roadside for group peeing and we were knackered at school next day.

All the resorts seemed the same, although at one you could ride a sad-looking flea-infested donkey on the only part of the beach that was too scruffy to put a deckchair. Mum wasn't having any of that and I have no idea which sandy option it was.

What they had in common was being great for small children like us. How we envied local kids who actually lived in those places. What a nuisance to have to go to school each day, but what wonderful weekends. Must be like permanently being on holiday.

I wondered if they would ever be tempted to go on a day outing to Chaulden. But I kept it to myself.

The resorts had everything. Punch and Judy shows all day long, buckets with battlement bottoms, spades and giant beach balls, all those different shells to collect from the water's edge and put in the shed until Mum chucked them out a fortnight later.

Noisy amusement arcades, just full of things to do. Put a coin in a slot, roll a penny, try to get a crane to grab a bar of chocolate. Sticks of rock, candyfloss, shellfish, maybe even a small funfair with dodgem cars, scary fast rides and music so loud you had to shout and shout.

It was fun, fun, fun all the way.

And maybe best of all, the inevitable fish and chips, always freshly-cooked and incredibly hot, eaten out of newspaper with a wooden fork, sitting on the sea wall as hopelessly hopeful seagulls hovered above, our plastic sandal-clad feet dangling in thin air. Happy, happy days.

Wherever we went, whatever we did, the success of the trip was measured (if only by the mums) purely by sunshine levels and the resultant ouch factor, itself dependant on the amount of skin peeling off our burnt faces, arms and backs during the following week.

Sun was good for you, sun made you go brown and therefore look so much better. Look at those pasty kids – don't they look ill, like they live in a cupboard?

OK, you couldn't bear anyone touching you because you were red raw, your clothes hurt, you couldn't even have a sheet on top of you so you couldn't sleep at night. No matter, what a great day that was.

You've never looked healthier – not like those people from that posh house in Boxmoor we met in the butcher's who spent a fortune going to some foreign country and came back the same colour as they went. What a total waste of money that was. Must have been pig sick.

No one had a sun hat or knew what suntan cream was, let alone bought any. The minute we set foot on sand, it was off with as much gear as was possible within the laws of decency.

Sunglasses, even the plastic ones they sold in Woolworth's, were for posing like film stars and shade was for the adults to sleep in during the afternoon. That's how it was.

"Get out and about, see the world, broaden your horizons." That's what Granda said.

Granda knew everything in the whole world, although he saw hardly any of it.

10
Christmas & Co

If I'd known then who Howard Carter was, I would assume the rear entrance to the Tudor Rose was rather like entering the tomb of Tutankhamun, as the archaeologist did in Egypt in 1922.

You got in through the side door nearest the community centre, Chaulden Hall, then down a couple of steps and through the pyramid-like gloom to another door into a tiny darkened chamber, in the corner of which was a till.

A couple of presses of the big white bell labelled PRESS (what else would you do) and reality resumed. The start of Christmas, about a week before the official kick-off.

Welcome to the inner sanctuary of Dad's local, the Tudor's off-sales, manned only intermittently by whoever had nothing better to do when the bell rang the other side of the wall in the public bar.

My job was to help carry the Christmas drinks back down the hill once the barman had worked his way through Dad's list. Depending who were to be this year's guests, grandparents along with real aunts and uncles calling in perhaps, and how much they had contributed to the final bill, the order went something like this:

Quarts of Whitbread pale and brown ales, Lemon Hart rum, Harvey's Bristol Cream sherry, R White's Cream Soda, Tizer, Johnnie Walker Scotch, Booth's gin, Captain Morgan rum, Stone's Original Green Ginger Wine, Warninks Advocaat, Babycham, Cherry B and any old lemon and orange squash.

We had to make two journeys.

Mum did all the fresh-food shopping on Christmas Eve, while Dad collected the turkey from the butcher, but by then we already had a load of 'essential' items which no one ever saw at other times.

A tin of Quality Street chocolates, Eat Me dates on a plastic stalk in a rounded oblong box, Epicure Pickled Walnuts, Politi's Turkish Delight covered in sugary cornflour, Jacob's Fig Rolls, a tin of giant Sun-Pat salted peanuts, Brazil nuts coated in chocolate, Callard & Bowser Butterscotch wrapped in luxurious golden foil and last, and most certainly least, a tin of Blue Bird toffees that were still there at Easter because no one really liked them.

Plus presents Mum kept so well hidden Sally and I would never find them. Normally behind all the half-empty tins of paint on the top shelf in the shed. Suddenly covered in unused sheets of sandpaper.

She bought all those on a spree two weeks earlier when the Chaulden Christmas Club paid out.

Every week, year round, I was sent just up the road to a house identical to ours with varying amounts of money and Mum's CCC card. The unwelcoming man sitting at his kitchen table shrouded in cigarette smoke put the cash in a large silver metal box and wrote the amount on the card, taking care not to knock over his bottle of Mann's Brown Ale.

As long as you had enough in credit, any sum could be withdrawn, for a small fee, anytime. Despite the CCC name, some people used it to fund summer holidays. Or indeed whenever they needed to get their hands back on their own cash. The neighbourhood bank at a time when hardly anyone had a personal bank account, it was a blessing for hundreds of households.

There were always stories of people running such clubs and then doing a runner themselves, with all the money. But we were in it for years, no problem.

Our money was earmarked for Mum to buy presents, to top up the box of decorations which lived in the attic and for Dad to get the vital ingredient: always a proper Christmas tree.

Some people were getting the terrible new fake ones, said Dad. Over his dead body. They were the sort of people who had plastic flowers on their dining room tables and electric fires in their living room grates.

One year, Dad came home a couple of days before Christmas not only with a lovely big very real tree, but one which was already decorated with a tree-topping fairy with wand, shiny baubles and dozens of tiny lights, complete with plug.

He'd got a bargain down the market, he explained, and everyone on the way home thought he was a real laugh holding it on the platform of the 320 bus like Father Christmas about to deliver it to needy children, smothered in pine needles.

Mum didn't laugh. She thought he'd got pissed at the King Harry pub (closed in 2006) by the bus station and by then the nearby stalls had run out of trees so he'd bought a shop's window display because he daren't come home without one.

Who knew? He didn't argue, that's for sure. It was a great tree, standing proudly in the corner of the living room and duly smothered in that tacky Lametta tinsel, with twisted crepe paper chains and fold-up Chinese lanterns all around, a blow-up Father Christmas dangling from the mirror, cards stuck with Sellotape to any spare bit of wood, everything from Woolworth's.

Everyone got all their Christmas bits and pieces from there. Everyone's living rooms looked much the same.

We usually had Christmas at home with Nanny and Granda, but sometimes went to Harlesden. We never went to Nanna and Grandad's in Wealdstone and they rarely came to us. Don't know why.

The pattern was much the same. It was a hive of activity from the moment they arrived around teatime on Christmas Eve when, like a magician pulling something out of his hat, Dad unveiled the drinks he'd carefully laid out on the top of the sideboard and covered with tea towels, maybe to avoid any premature temptation.

Beers for the men (a 'drop of short' was promised for later), gins for the women. Fizzy pop for Sally and me. All with lots of sandwiches, sausage rolls, pork pie and pickles, peanuts, dates, chocolates and fruit. Then an early night. Big day tomorrow. Don't want to spoil it. You need your beauty sleep.

The Big Day started with a pillowcase full of goodies which Father Christmas had kindly left on the bottom of our beds during the night without disturbing us. I believed in him until I was about seven, I think. But don't tell your sister, or you'll ruin everything. And get nothing.

The goodies had a welcome familiar feel to them – more nuts, mandarin oranges, large tube of Smarties, Dinky car, jigsaw, gold-wrapped chocolate pennies and a fiendishly difficult puzzle made out of twisted bits of metal.

The annual and uninspired scrambled eggs on toast out of the way, it was on to the Christmas tree and its surrounding bigger presents where Dad loomed large with a helpful pair of scissors.

As he handed them out and we ripped the packages apart, Mum sat on the floor with a pencil and paper, trying to jot down who'd bought what for who so she could then nag us well into January about writing thankyou letters. What a chore that was.

But of all the lovely things I got over the years the best present ever wasn't the biggest or anywhere near the most expensive.

It was the year Granda took me on the top deck of a No. 8 London bus all the way along Oxford Street and on to Gamages in High Holborn, the toyshop of dreams (it closed in 1972) with an 800ft train set running through it. I think I was about six.

He bought me a large chocolate mint mouse in green and silver foil which I ate on the way home and a Marx Toys clockwork climbing fireman who always fell backwards off his yellow two-piece ladder when he got halfway up and I had to wind him up and start again.

When we were at home, Mum got up early to put The Bird (never called the turkey, for reasons completely unknown) in the oven before breakfast. The meal was scheduled for 2pm.

It was smothered in Cookeen with Paxo sage and onion stuffing duly stuffed within and a few chipolatas dotted around, destined to be submerged in fat, like pork submarines.

For about seven hours, it was dragged in and out of the oven, fat spooned over it, a fork frequently plunged into it as though to make sure it really was deceased.

The sole aim was for the perfect bird and it was always heralded as such by the grateful assembled company, never ever described as anything other than moist and delicious, although it was always dry, crumbly and almost completely tasteless.

It was to be accompanied by roast potatoes, carrots and, for the only time in the year, Brussels sprouts. No one liked them, but you had to have them. Come on, it's Christmas. Don't be silly, eat up. Good for you.

All prepared long before breakfast, after which the sherry and beer drinking started, the new toys were properly introduced to their new owners and the radio was turned up so we could all enjoy the lovely Christmas music as selected by the BBC.

And so to dinner. The same as a Sunday dinner, but with hats. Silly paper hats unravelled from a Woolworth's cracker. Hats which defied all known logic by being unable to fit any head anywhere in the world.

Worse, no sooner had you vainly attempted to secure the hat on your ill-suited head, you were obliged to read out an accompanying 'joke'. What do elves learn at school? The elf-abet. Who hides in a baker's at Christmas? A mince spy. How those sides ached.

By which time, of course, your dinner was stone cold. Is that why everyone always preferred Boxing Day dinner, when the turkey was actually meant to be cold?

At 3pm we all had to listen to the Queen's Speech on the radio, no matter what. Stop everything. Concentrate. Her Majesty was talking to all her subjects, all over the British Empire, not just us English, although we were obviously the most important.

Every single one of them was listening. It was the greatest body of people in the world, the greatest empire the world has ever known, said Granda, standing rigidly.

No one disagreed, but it was still incredibly boring for everyone, not just us kids. But we had to listen. It was the Queen and she was a very nice lady. You wouldn't hear from her again until next year, just see her in the paper now and then opening some shops, going to factories perhaps, looking at rows of soldiers, bending down to take small bunches of nearly-dead flowers from shy little girls and cracking bottles on the front of big ships and wasting all the wine.

No sooner had the Queen done her bit, than the washing-up began, inevitably followed by the adult sleep-in.

The evening sarnies, cakes and once-a-year treats were welcome, but night time was music time. Always, always, Mum played the piano even if there were only six of us there. As long as the sheet music was somewhere within that old cardboard box she kept under the stool, she could play anything.

But she stuck to the traditional singalong songs, like Roll Out The Barrel, On Mother Kelly's Doorstep, Daisy Daisy, Happy Days Are Here Again, Pack Up Your Troubles, You Are My Sunshine, My Old Man Said Follow The Van, Down At The Old Bull And Bush, Bye Bye Blackbirds, Danny Boy, Maybe It's Because I'm A Londoner and, of course, Show Me The Way To Go Home. Even if we were already.

We looked over her shoulder to sing along to the words on the sheet music, taking care not to knock over her gin and orange squash or spill our own drinks into the ashtray.

Or, even worse, all over the inevitable new blouse that Dad bought her every year from a shop near The Bell pub in the old town that specialised in clothes for mature women and made her look the spitting image of Jayne Mansfield, he reckoned. Who?

The old-time favourites came thick and fast and in no particular order, the volume increasing as surely as the stock from the Tudor Rose off-sales diminished.

But no matter what, there was always the star turn.

As if being introduced to a Royal Albert Hall audience for a night of carols by candlelight, rather than a few family members in a brightly-lit council house, Granda would suddenly but slowly rise from his chair, his arms straight by his sides, chest out.

The signal for Mum to sit back, her piano keys temporarily redundant, as he began to sing, all of us completely transfixed despite knowing precisely what was coming next.

From deep within himself he produced Silent Night (Stille Nacht) in German, just as he sang it last year and the year before that – and all those years ago, linking arms with his fellow prisoners and guards in the hellish Great War prison camp, none of them having any idea what the future held for them. If anything at all.

"Stille Nacht, heilige Nacht,
Alles schläft; einsam wacht
Nur das traute hochheilige Paar.
Holder Knabe im lockigen Haar,
Schlaf in himmlischer Ruh!
Schlaf in himmlischer Ruh!"

It's the only music that still brings a tear to my eye. What could have been going through his mind as he sang? If only he had chosen to share it with us. But he didn't. He never did. Granda would share his knowledge, offer his opinions, give his help and advice to anyone at any time.

But he chose never to share his emotions. He was a book that was at once open, but before you knew it, was firmly closed. No one ever knew the Granda within. That's how it was.

If Silent Night was the low point of Christmas, in its unique way for our family, the high point was never far behind. The grand finale, the roof-lifter, the… whatever.

Of all the songs, none was sung more loudly, with more feeling, more – I never knew what – than the adopted anthem of the Labour Party. The Red Flag, written by Irish socialist journalist Jim Connell in 1889, just a few years before Granda was born.

As the final drinks were downed, Mum hit those piano keys for the last time of the night and they all belted it out to the tune of the traditional German carol, O Tannenbaum (The Fir Tree):

"The people's flag is deepest red,
It shrouded oft our martyred dead.
And ere their limbs grew stiff and cold,
Their hearts' blood dyed to every fold.

Then raise the scarlet standard high,
Beneath its folds we'll live and die.
Though cowards flinch and traitors sneer,
We'll keep the Red Flag flying here."

The singing had barely died down before Mum was busy on next year's Christmas card list, ruthlessly noting those who had failed to oblige this time so that they would save her the stamp money in future.

Of course, no one ever mentioned sending a card to The Woman Downstairs, although that clearly wouldn't involve any postage expenditure and would be a nice thing to do. Probably.

I hope she wasn't angry about being ignored like that. It worried me a lot, all through Boxing Day every year, which was much the same as Christmas Day except we'd already opened the presents and we had bubble and squeak.

BONFIRE NIGHT was second only to Christmas in the kids' fun calendar and the weeks leading up to the crescendo of flashes, bangs and wallops in back gardens everywhere were fondly anticipated just as much as November 5 itself.

Every spare bit of money went on fireworks in the shop at the end of Boxmoor, where every year the owner opened a special room out the back loaded with goodies, mainly from the local Brock's Fireworks factory, just outside Hemel at Cupid Green. It closed in 1971.

Others came from their rival northern company, Standard, or the long-established Surrey firm, Pain's, said to have unwittingly supplied the explosives for the Gunpowder Plot of 1605 from their original home in London's East End which did, after all, get things all fired up.

We started buying them in September, fascinated by the rows of brightly-wrapped explosives and their exciting names. Silver Rain, Chrysanthemum Fountain, Jack In The Box, Astra Floodlight, Mine Of Serpents, Jewelled Pyramid, Volcano, Olympic Torch, Flying Saucer and the rest.

But mostly bangers and rockets, the real deal.

Not that we saved them all for Bonfire Night, anything but. Despite dire warnings of getting your hand blown off by misuse (no one ever did), penny bangers were lit on the doorsteps of the unsuspecting while we tore off up the road. Rockets were fired from milk bottles and aimed at school buildings, Catherine wheels nailed to any vulnerable fences.

To get even more fireworks, we went begging at the railway station with our Guy. Made from an old pair of trousers and a shirt and stuffed with newspaper, he was propped up on the wall outside the ticket office in the hope that passengers would show their financial approval of our ingenuity.

And amazingly they always did, their pennies dropped into our seaside bucket, the one with an octopus on.

His work done, Guy was ceremoniously cremated on a bonfire on November 5 while the fireworks he'd sportingly helped to secure went off all around him.

The night itself was seemingly always foggy, freezing or wet – or a truly uncomfortable combination of all three. Not even the Batchelors chicken soup poured from a thermos flask and the sausage sandwiches could disguise the chill. But never mind, it was pure excitement.

Most times, it happened in our back garden. Dad would buy a small selection box of Brock's and get everything prepared before it got dark, digging a small hole in which to place the more powerful fireworks and giving us sparklers to wave patterns in the night sky.

If not at home, it was in someone else's back garden nearby. Everyone, but everyone, joined in and everyone had a bonfire. It seemed as though Chaulden was on fire and next morning the streets were littered with the wooden sticks of expired rockets, the smell of cordite still filling the nostrils as we walked to school, eager to exchange stories.

Once we went to Boxmoor for an organised display on the field at the end of the village by the Roman Catholic church of St Mary and St Joseph. Dad liked that best because he didn't have to let off all the fireworks and he could go over the road for a pint in the Three Blackbirds. Mum wasn't so keen.

EASTER time was chocolate time and a couple of weeks off school. We got a ridiculous amount of eggs of all shapes and sizes, mainly representing the output of Rowntree's, Nestles and Fry's, given to us by grandparents, real aunts and real uncles and locally-adopted 'aunties'.

Most came in square boxes with a window at the front, the eggs themselves wrapped in patterned foil. Some came rammed in mugs embellished with racing cars or Mickey Mouse designs, so Sally and I would just take out the egg, get the foil off and stick the mug in the back of the cupboard with all those from previous years, none of them ever to be used.

The best ones had small chocolates inside, like Smarties and Cadbury's Chocolate Buttons. You could eat the little bagful and keep the shell of the egg for later.

Much later. The chocolate stash always lasted until summer, stacked in a corner of the larder like we were expecting a siege.

Hot cross buns were a brilliant treat, too, piping hot out of the oven and drowned in Anchor Butter so it oozed all over your hands. They were only in the shops for a few days, never available any other time.

Best of all, though – the chicken. If turkey was Christmas, chicken was Easter and far, far better. Lovely crisp skin, flesh with real flavour and, of course, the normal Sunday roast veg. A true once-a-year treat all the kids we knew looked forward to. Even the ones whose mums could cook the rest of the time.

As far as religion goes, Easter meant absolutely nothing in our house, although we always got a card from Real Aunty Brenda with a picture of Jesus hanging on a cross. Every year he looked totally different, apart from having a beard.

Which always made me wonder. If he really was the most important man ever, how come the card makers couldn't make up their minds who he really was?

It was the only card we ever got.

Every year, Dad put it behind the bread bin.

BIRTHDAYS meant presents, but nothing like Christmas. You didn't even get a day off school because it was your birthday. Just a few family gifts, maybe clothes and things for school, nothing exciting. The only important thing about your birthday was being a whole year older.

It felt great. No kid in the world ever wanted to be younger again.

I can remember a Craft Master painting by numbers kit, which came in a really big box, but not much else springs to mind. And that was pretty boring, like a colouring book really.

The lid of the box showed various African animals having a drink in a river with a bright yellow canoe tethered to a tree nearby.

It was like they were about to finish their drinks and then jump in it and paddle furiously upstream into a torrent, over a giant waterfall and heroically emerge in the calm waters of the back of beyond, serenaded by smiling crocodiles playing guitars.

You filled in all the outlined areas marked 3, for instance, which coincided with a tiny plastic pot of paint similarly numbered. It went all over your fingers the minute you loosened the rather challenging lid.

You were then supposed to wait for that to dry before moving on to adjacent different numbered areas and their different paints. No one could wait that long, of course, so it ended up a big runny mess.

No matter the presents, there were always the birthday parties and they were never anything other than good.

I had a couple at home and lots more in other friends' houses. They followed almost exactly the same pattern and the star of the show was always the same: banana sandwiches. How I loved them, all sweet and soggy. And a bit of chocolate cake, of course. And maybe some animal-shaped biscuits with icing you licked off first.

The rest of the food never varied from meat paste, fish paste and the sickly white-iced birthday cake adorned with a suitable number of candles and a random plastic boyish thing, usually a racing car, sunk into the goo. Maybe a few sausage rolls, a bit of pork pie. Followed by jelly and ice-cream. Every time.

We played the same classic games. Pass the Parcel, scattering newspaper all around the room until someone won a packet of sweet cigarettes or some such. Nothing any more exciting than that. Musical Statues, at which everyone but everyone cheated. And Blind Man's Bluff, the birthday boy inevitably being given the leading role.

There were always a couple of girls there, but they just sat about in new frocks and cardigans.

The only deviation to all those birthday party regulations was the day we went to Keith's house in the next estate, Warners End. Mum knew his mum, Peggy, because they'd worked together in Wealdstone, cleaning offices. Only for top people, of course.

But Keith's dad, Eddie, had just bought the greatest thing ever – a Grundig tape recorder with a microphone on a long lead. The machine was about the size of a small suitcase. None of us had ever seen one before, let alone be able to watch it working and hear our own voices.

One by one, we all had to say our names and then we had to sing Happy Birthday To You together. We watched the tape reels go round and round and then Uncle Eddie played it all back.

It was simply unbelievable. None of us wanted to go home.

I told Mum and Dad about it, but they said it as just a fad some people were going through.

The other birthday treat in the Riches household was being able to choose your own tea at home. You could have whatever you liked, that was the rule. Anything in the whole wide world. In other words, the Co-op in Chaulden.

I opted for exactly the same for as many birthdays as I can remember. Thin slices of cold bread-crumbed cooked ham with a fried egg and chips. And bread and butter, of course.

Mum did the chips in a big frying pan full of lard because we didn't have a chip pan. We were about to get one, apparently, before No. 25 Long Chaulden went up in flames.

Well, some of it anyway. One evening, Mum at No. 25 took her eye off the game and the fat in her pan burst into flames as she was doing their tea. Pan-demonium, Dad reckoned, delighted at his own wit.

Two fire engines! Sirens! Police cars! Flashing lights! Squirting hosepipes! Such excitement! Loads and loads of smoke blowing down the road, water everywhere and the street full of people just standing about staring and nodding like they knew everything. A whole load of them even got off a bus to have a look.

It was fantastic.

The kitchen was gutted, the whole place was smoke-damaged. It meant the couple and their two boys, older than us, couldn't stay. So they got re-housed on another estate. Never saw them again.

And never got a chip pan.

"Kitchens are dangerous places, son. You're playing with fire and that has to be respected, just like water." That's what Granda said.

Granda knew everything in the whole world, although he never cooked anything in his life.

11
Up To The Juniors

Schooldays are the happiest days of your life, I was told at least a thousand times. An incredibly stupid thing to say, when you think about it, especially to someone leaving school convinced that life from then on is destined to be a major disappointment.

But my school really was a great place to be. Everyone loved it. There was no class disruption because there was absolute respect for the teachers, like my first one in the juniors, Miss Simmons. No one answered back, no one took sickies.

No one had even heard the word bullying, although we did get told off once for surrounding Owen in the playground and chanting the rhyme: "Taffy was a Welshman, Taffy was a thief. Taffy came to my house and stole a piece of beef."

The encircled Owen didn't mind at all, in fact he happily joined in and liked being the centre of attention for once, but it wasn't nice said Miss Simmons so we didn't do it again.

Any dodgy behaviour, perhaps answering back or looking out of the window, and you had to stand near the door and face the wall. So there was hardly any. Certainly no junior school teacher ever smacked a child, no need. A few of them had a shout, but that's all. That's how it was.

The fun element aside, going up to Big School, or Next Door, as everyone called it (because it was) was a real big deal for a boy still nearly a month away from being a whole eight years old despite having three years of schooling behind him. I was nervous, I think, of the unknown. I couldn't remember that ever being on my list of emotions.

To mark the occasion of the switch from Chaulden Mixed Infant School to the adjoining Chaulden Mixed Junior School, I had a brand new leather satchel bought somewhere in Wealdstone. Mum had picked it while out shopping with Nanna, who'd paid for it. But whatever you do, don't tell Grandad of course.

In it went Dad's old wooden pencil case, his only remaining link from his own young past. He'd set fire to everything else the minute he left school, he said, but had saved this especially for the son he knew he'd have one day. He handed it over like it was a family heirloom, which I suppose it was, in a way. There weren't any other heirlooms hanging around the house, that's for sure.

I slid back the top piece and in its belly plonked a brand-new rubber and two pencils.

Dad said I had to have a regular pencil and a soft pencil. He explained the difference at some length, but I lost it somewhere. One was HB, best for writing, the other a soft 2B, apparently better for sketching. Not that I ever differentiated, to be honest.

They both looked the same, but the 2B needed more attention from the other box inhabitant, a sharpener. Basically a razor blade safely enclosed in a small metal box in case you were tempted to use a knife and took a finger off. Or someone else's.

One thing that would never accompany them was a ballpoint pen. It may have been boom time for these relatively new arrivals on the stationery scene, but not here. They were banned by the school until the fourth year. Not good enough to help you write properly was the thought.

From day one at the juniors, there were two major differences.

For the first time, we had assembly every morning. Teacher would stand at the front of the class holding the register, a giant red notebook, call out our names one by one and tick us off when we responded "Present". If we didn't answer loudly enough, she said we'd go down as absent. Even if we weren't. So we shouted rather than call her bluff.

Then we'd walk in a tight line along the short corridor into the juniors' school hall to meet up with all the other classes, us smaller ones sitting cross-legged on the floor at the front near the wall bars which we used for PE.

But not all of us. One girl and one boy had to stay behind at their desks and read all by themselves. A dinner lady came into the classroom every morning and sat near the door. She was only keeping an eye on the pair of them, but it looked for all the world like she was preventing any attempt at escape.

They were Roman Catholics, whatever that meant. At no stage was it properly explained to us, but it was something to do with Jesus and history and not really believing in the same things. What it meant for now was they weren't allowed in assembly with the rest of us, so that made them outcasts for their whole time at junior school. They didn't even seem to join in things during playtime. That's how it was.

Assembly began with a hymn. Mrs Jones would play the piano over in the corner, staring hard at the sheet music in front of her. Whatever it was, the tune always sounded much the same, but the words were different. I think all the songs came out of the same hymn book which was hundreds of years old, something like:

"Lord of all hopefulness,
Lord of all joy,
Whose trust, ever child-like,
No cares can destroy.
Be there at our waking
And give us, we pray,
Your bliss in our hearts, Lord,
At the break of the day."

We all enjoyed a sing-song, no matter what the material, but a teacher went round the hall looking up and down the rows, just in case we'd somehow suddenly lost that enthusiasm, to make sure everyone was joining in.

After that, Mr Chapman, the Headmaster, came round the corner from his study and talked to us for a bit about what was going on in the school, how we should all try our hardest all the time, stop chucking food on the canteen floor or 'spoiling' the toilets, those sort of things. Never anything interesting.

We finished up all kneeling and reciting the Lord's Prayer before traipsing out, row by row in strict age group order, back to our classrooms for the lessons to begin.

The most significant change, miles more important than assembly, was learning to write properly. Until now, writing meant slowly drawing letters on paper in a designated way and in a certain order to form simple words.

We'd been given the basics. How to hold the pencil properly. How to make all the individual letters distinct from the rest. Above all, how to be neat and tidy. All our work looked much the same.

But now, all of a sudden, all that was to change. We were going to learn how to write like grown-ups, with all the letters within a word joined together. Every morning, we'd spend time on the learning process and by the end of this year or next, said optimistic Miss Simmons, we would have no further need for our pencils.

What's more, once we'd mastered the basics, we would go on to develop our own styles of handwriting. No one wrote the same as anyone else, even though they used the same letters to form the same words. Just as we all had similar-looking hands and fingers, but no two people had identical fingerprints.

Wonderful. I absolutely loved it. A major turning point in my life.

Instead of the pencil, we were each given a new nib pen, basically a small piece of wood with a sharp metal nib on the end. It sat in a special holder on our desks and was not to be left anywhere else. Or else. Next to it was the inkwell, a Bakelite pot sunk into the desk and filled from a small watering can which contained navy blue ink powder, mixed with water.

The wells had been filled for us today, but from now on that was a job for us. Or at least one of us at a time. We'd take it in turns to be Ink Monitor, on duty for a few days to save everyone else getting covered in ink during the rather messy topping-up process. It would be carried out during morning playtime.

Teacher went through the entire alphabet on the blackboard, writing all the letters we were familiar with, but each of which had now grown two tails so they could be linked to others. It was called cursive script, but always referred to more simply as joined-up writing. Either way, it was brilliant.

We dripped ink all over our desks and all over the paper in our new notebooks, of course we did, but we were given a helping hand in the form of sheets of magical blotting paper to mop it up, so that was all right.

As we got better, the dripping became less of an issue. But our hands were still permanently covered with ink stains and our shirts beyond a perfect wash.

Those mid-morning sessions weren't nearly long enough for me and I wanted to take a pen and one of the spare inkwells home so I could write and write after school, but teacher wouldn't let me although I promised to bring them back every day.

I asked Mum and Dad to help, but they weren't really interested in what I did at school as long as I didn't get into trouble. So instead of writing I just went out and played football in the road.

Each class in the juniors was split into four houses – Jupiter (green), Saturn (red), Mercury (yellow) and Neptune (blue).

Presumably this was to help make us competitive, but it only really came into play once a year, on Sports Day, when everyone in the whole school had to wear a suitably-coloured ribbon and be ushered into four rope-ringed sections along the length of the 100-yard course.

Parents were seated on the opposite side, each of them also given the appropriate ribbon as they filed through the school gates in the hope of fostering some sort of allegiance.

Not that there were many of them since most had to go to work on a midweek afternoon, like Mum and Dad.

Suitably corralled, and waiting our own turns to perform, we'd then be expected to shout hysterically in favour of someone from another class we'd barely set eyes on who had randomly been chosen for us as a housemate. Even if they were destined to be last. Which was often the case with us Jupiters, but not me. I always did OK as a sprinter.

I was less impressive at the other Sports Day events, particularly the silly ones like the egg and spoon, three-legged and sack races which just degenerated into a human bundle. No one ever avoided falling over in those sacks. Fun, though.

Cricket ball throwing was more taxing for me and similarly unsuccessful, but the real sticking point were the sandpit events – high jump, long jump and the very challenging hop, step and jump.

And I mean sticking. The entire sandpit was always full of carefully-concealed cat shit, no matter how regularly it was raked. It put everyone off. Still, couldn't complain – it made a change from the dog shit found everywhere else in Chaulden.

Back in the classroom, we ditched the house distinctions for another year or so, but were becoming much more competitive and every day encouraged to be so.

Everyone battled to get things stuck on the wall, no matter what. It was a sort of gallery of excellence, I suppose.

Apart from the usual drawings and examples of neat writing, the wall and its random shelving accommodated all the things we made in art and crafts – papier-maché cars, ships and planes, neatly-stitched table mats featuring assorted animals, balsa wood space rockets and rag dolls stuffed with shredded newspaper.

There was a special large area reserved for kites, which we made from long thin pieces of wood to which we stuck a piece of wallpaper we'd been told to bring from home (but not if it's still attached to the wall, children!) and a ball of string.

In reality, none of the kites took off, despite us all charging round and round the playground dragging them behind, but it didn't really matter. They looked great on the wall and lessons like those were fondly anticipated, especially when us boys made our own wooden train set, with our initials painted on the carriages, none of which looked like any other. It was almost the length of the classroom.

While we created our own railway, the girls did knitting and sewing and some were even allowed to go into the canteen to see how the ladies in there managed to cook the dinners. No boys were, but then they weren't going to become housewives, were they, explained teacher.

The most obvious sign of progress was the giant Gold Star Chart, there on the back of the classroom door for all to see all the time. Every piece of work we did was marked by teacher, who may – but mostly may not – then draw a star, or two, at the end of the picture/writing/sums, along with suitably encouraging words.

If you found you'd got a star on your work when it was returned to you, you went back to teacher at playtime who'd give you a sticky-backed gold star from a packet of them in her desk drawer which you could then lick and fix on the Gold Star Chart alongside your name. Some had dozens of stars, some would finish the whole year with one or two.

An instant way of seeing who was top and who was bottom. A constant reminder of your classroom status, whether you wanted to be reminded or not.

I think I always realised I was one of the lucky ones at Chaulden Juniors.

Not only did I like school, made lots of friends and genuinely wanted to learn new things, I didn't find the work difficult. But even so the teachers were not exactly generous with praise.

My first annual report, in spring 1959, said I was "Often careless"... "Inclined to hurry"... "Good when he makes the effort."

It was by some miracle, then, that I managed to finish second out of 107 pupils in the year group. Dad said Jesus Christ must have been the clear winner.

Second! A rare C grade was for music. It should have been a CC because I was Completely Clueless at playing a tambourine or a recorder, so they wouldn't let me anywhere near a proper instrument. Not that we had any that I recall, although a few older girls were given piano lessons in the school hall. No boys, never knew why.

The morning hymn included, I loved singing, but I suspect I was just as bad at that, especially when we all sat on the shiny wooden floor of the junior school hall to listen to the radio once a week.

The School Broadcasting Council, set up in 1947, was an arm of the BBC, feeding radio programmes specifically to pupils like us all over Britain.

The Singing Together show, presented on Monday mornings for many years by William Appleby, was a highlight of the week for eight out of 10 schools in the country, including us. It didn't end until 2004.

We'd all belt out a sea shanty as the radio provided expert accompaniment way beyond the talent of our own Mrs Jones:

"What shall we do with the drunken sailor,
What shall we do with the drunken sailor,
What shall we do with the drunken sailor
Ear-lye in the morning?"

Or maybe some traditional old English song:

*"Oh there was a little drummer
And he loved a one-eyed cook.
And he loved her, oh he loved her
Though she had a cock-eyed look.
With her one eye in the pot
And the other up the chimney,
With a bow-wow-wow,
Fal-lal the dow-a-diddy
Bow-wow-wow."*

And very often the favourite among us boys:

*"There was an old man
Named Michael Finnegan,
He had whiskers
On his chin-ne-gan.
The wind blew them off
And blew them on again.
Poor old Michael Finnegan,
Begin Again.*

*"There was an old man
Named Michael Finnegan,
Heard this song
And began to sing again.
Hurt my ears
So don't begin again.
And that's the end of
Michael Finnegan!"*

We were encouraged to sing as loudly as possible, presumably at the expense of any choral excellence, and tried our hardest to drown out the few fourth-year kids standing up the front who were trying, vainly, to accompany the songs on their recorders by way of their music lesson. But us singers were always too slow or too fast. They never had a chance.

"Music's a wonderful thing. Without music, the world would be a sorry place." That's what Granda said.
Granda knew everything in the whole world, although the only music he liked was really old, like him.

12
Away From School

My closest friend, also called Steve (there were five Steves in the year group), was usually alongside me whenever we were freed from our rows of desks to do things like painting and modelling, and in the playground and out of school we were rarely separated.

I loved going to Steve's house, all of 150 yards away, where we played with toy soldiers in his back garden at 121 Northridge Way.

We had a few of the old heavy lead ones between us, many of them with limbs or heads missing in courageous neighbourhood action, but most were plastic and we hid them behind large stones or within the areas of uncut grass, which was always alive with grasshoppers when it was dry, frogs when it wasn't. The occasional toad, perhaps, that most unlovable of creatures, an amphibian reminder of revolting Uncle Lionel.

Most fun came from the die-cast artillery cannon, a spring-loaded field gun about Dinky size (but made by the London firm of Britains Ltd) which could fire spent matchsticks a couple of feet or so.

Accuracy wasn't its strongpoint and realistically you had to be about two inches away to stand a chance of knocking over a soldier, even a wobbly lightweight plastic one.

Lots of my soldiers were Japanese, bought by the bagful from the newsagent's, especially the crouching ones with flaps down the back of their peaked caps. I suppose that was to keep the sun off their necks in the jungles of Borneo and thereabouts, although you'd have thought bullets were more of a problem. I called them all Tojo, since I was a bit short on other Japanese names.

Once we irritatingly hid in the bushes when Steve's mum and my mum's best friend, Aunty Laura, called us in for tea. She shouted and shouted but couldn't see us.

When we eventually went in, she made us eat all the fried beef sausages that were by now burnt to a crisp because of us and slapped the back of his legs.

I was all right, you weren't allowed to slap other people's kids unless they were really naughty. Then it was OK, as long as you didn't hit them too hard. I don't think anyone ever slapped me.

They remain the best sausages I've ever tasted. And they came with the inevitable bread and butter – but with a big difference. They had ready-sliced and wrapped Wonderloaf, like everyone in Chaulden except us. Dad said he'd never eat what he called plastic bread. Nor did he. What next? Teabags instead of real tea? Don't be daft.

And with the sausages came a big helping of hot Heinz Baked Beans, something Mum would never let us have at home because she thought they didn't have any goodness, not like her meat and two veg.

Spam was another no-no, although all the other kids often had it for tea, mainly as fritters. And with those very same beans in a supporting role. Cat food from America that was forced on the troops during the War, dropped by parachutes to those on the front line, poor buggers, Dad reckoned. Not that he ever tried Spam. Or cat food, as far as I know.

Steve's back garden was rather more confined than our other favourite playground. The Grand Union Canal stretched all the way along the bottom of the playing fields beneath the railway embankment, a watery wonderland we took full advantage of as we got more adventurous, more regularly venturing off the estate.

Nowhere else in the whole of Hemel was deemed by parents as being potentially more dangerous for children than the canal. And nowhere else provided such a magnetic attraction for people of all ages.

It was best for us there when it was really foggy, which was lots of the time. Ideal for pretending to be Royal Marines huddled together by the shore, peering through the camouflaging murk waiting to be picked up by a landing craft after a desperate kill-or-be-killed mission behind enemy lines.

Handily, the phantom craft always managed to navigate its way through coastal defences and secure our safety just in time to leg it back along the towpath in time for tea.

The kids' paddling pool by the Fishery Inn Bridge over the canal was a magnet for the likes of us, fed by the River Bulbourne as it flowed along to its marriage with the River Gade a mile away at Two Waters and onwards hand in hand towards Apsley, Kings Langley and Watford before joining the River Colne near Rickmansworth.

The river itself was rich with sticklebacks and minnows, sometimes a stray gudgeon or two and maybe a perch, which we all hated because of its prickly spines. A nightmare to release from our nylon nets, which were otherwise used to collect any number of frogs, tipped into our buckets but always released when it was time to go home.

Our friend Robert had bad luck by that pool. He took his wellies off because his feet were hot and went in the water for a paddle. But when he got out and put a boot back on, it was full of wasps. Thanks to a stray bit of ice-lolly attracting the unloved beasts, we all later assumed.

He yelled and yelled and someone from the Fishery pub came out and took him to the casualty department at the hospital. He had two days off school and his mum went potty because he shouldn't have been there. Never mind the state of his foot, he wasn't allowed near the canal before he could swim. Served him right, she said, won't be going down there again.

An equally risky pastime in that part of the canal was skimming stones at the commercial barges and chucking things at the ferocious-looking young bargees aboard them.

There was a constant stream of barges, either bringing coal or other heavy bulky items up from London for points along the canal as far as Aylesbury, or else pure lime juice to be processed by the Rose's company based at Boxmoor Wharf. At its busiest, there were 25,000 barrels stored there, making it the biggest lime juice depot in the world. It closed in 1983.

The Aylesbury-bound barges would have to slow down as they approached the locks the other side of the Fishery Bridge, so having hurled lumps of mud in their direction, we now had to run off and hide in nearby woods in case the bargees jumped ship and came after us.

Sometimes we went further afield for playtime by the water – to the gravel pits near the canal at Winkwell, home of the famous hand-operated (until 1984) swing bridge by the Three Horseshoes pub, a mile or so away towards Berkhamsted and the furthest we were supposed to stray from home.

There were big Keep Out notices all around the Westbrook Mere pits, but since it was owned by Dad's fishing club we thought it fair enough to scale the fences out of sight of the warden. We were only tree-climbing, after all, seeing who could get furthest out on the branches overhanging the water without actually touching it. Or falling in. It happened.

For all the canal and its delightful surroundings had to offer, none of my friends had any particular interest in rod-and-line fishing. Me neither, which was a great shame for Dad, whose life it was every Sunday in the coarse season. Which meant all year except the close season, March 15-June 15 on all rivers.

No matter what the weather, he never missed a week by a riverbank or lake unless we were away from home. That, darts night and a weekend pub visit, were set in stone. Otherwise, he did much as he was told.

He got up at ridiculous hours to be picked up outside the house by a friend who had a car or, most often, by the Boxmoor & District Angling Society coach, which looked like it was held together by old bits of fishing line and had never seen a new coat of paint.

By the sound of it, the engine wasn't up to much, either. It made noises like those cars you see at the circus with clowns sitting in them until they explode and all the doors fall off.

I never went on those trips, although a lot of the sons of Dad's workmates did, which must have made it worse for him. But I did try hard to get enthusiastic.

He took me to the canal several times to show me what to do. He bought me a special small boy's rod with all the bits and pieces. Showed me how to tie on hooks, floats and weights, how to cast, what to do if I caught something.

That didn't help. I caught a small flappy thing on one visit. Dad showed me how to reel it in, slowly and carefully, and there it was. Right in front of me, a hook stuck in its lip. As instructed, I had to grasp the slippery flappy thing in my bare hands, get the hook out and drop it gently back in the water.

It was an awful experience, worse even than being shown how to get the hook through the head of a live and wriggling maggot, among hundreds kept in a box under Dad's stool, which attracted the flappy thing in the first place.

It just wasn't for me. Fish-catching aside, it involved too long by the water with absolutely nothing happening. You just sat there, which must have been a treat if you were on your feet in a factory for 48 hours a week, but not much of a lure away from the action for the likes of me.

I simply couldn't stay quiet, or sit still, long enough.

Encouraged by Mum, at least I often helped Dad with his fishing gear in the kitchen on a Saturday night, sorting out hooks into their size-related compartments in his special tackle box, re-taping rod eyes, re-varnishing his home-made floats and smoothing down the cork rod handles with sandpaper.

I really enjoyed all that Dad-son bonding. Much more involvement than actually going fishing. I still felt like I'd let him down, mind.

I always waited in anticipation when the coach pulled up outside the house on Sunday evenings. Dad hauled himself off with all his gear, but it was only rarely that the wetbag he carried over his shoulder contained that dream of a catch – a live eel.

When he had one, he would call out as he came down the steps and walked past the kitchen window, to enable horrified Mum and Sally time to escape into the living room. Then I'd watch, fascinated, as he went through his routine.

He half-filled our biggest cooking pot with cold water and put it on the stove to boil, leaving the tap running to fill the kitchen sink. Then he pulled on his thick gloves, got his ferocious meat cleaver off its hook in the larder, then gently tipped the eel into the sink from his bag.

As it started to wriggle, he grasped the eel by the neck, lifted it out of the sink onto the draining board, then chopped it in chunks with the cleaver, pushing the still-wriggling pieces back into the cold water.

When the pot came to the boil, he transferred the pieces from the sink, replaced the lid and let them bubble away while he cleared up all the blood and guts and told Mum it was safe to return.

She never lifted that lid. He did, though, and we'd eat half of the chunks hot with mashed spuds, vinegar and pepper and a slice of dry bread. The other bits were left to cool in the pan overnight, creating their own jelly. The best jellied eels I've ever tasted.

Sometimes, I'd have a small bowl of them for breakfast. But if anyone at school asked what I had, I'd say Sugar Puffs in case they thought we were a family of weirdos.

"Stewed eels, jellied eels, smoked eels, you can't beat eels." That's what Granda said.

Granda knew everything in the whole world, although his daily stew never had any eels in it.

13
The World Of Reading

Janet and John aside, comics were chiefly responsible for kicking off my devotion to the written word, especially as we moved through junior years two and three.

What better way to be drawn to the joys of the language than by stunning pictures and comic strips, stories of pure fun and adventure to stretch any imagination in an easy-to-read format of ideal length that has never been bettered.

There were two stand-out publications, both produced by the family firm of DC Thomson in Dundee, and both delivered to our door every week, where they never failed to be read from cover to cover.

The Dandy's undoubted star was the monstrous cow-pie muncher Desperate Dan, who ate enough at one sitting to feed Chaulden. On the cover was Korky the Cat, providing the cartoonish pet interest and the other pages were filled with unlikely tales of Keyhole Kate (from the first issue in 1937), accident-prone Smasher and the rest.

But for me, The Beano just shaded it thanks to Dennis the Menace (now, he was a proper toe rag), Minnie the Minx, Little Plum, Roger the Dodger and, the best of all comic characters ever, The Bash Street Kids featuring Plug, Sidney, Smiffy, Danny, Erbert, Fatty, Toots and Spotty. The strip was originally called When The Bell Rings.

I also read the likes of The Beezer (twice the paper size of other comics, top reads being Calamity Jane and The Numskulls), The Hotspur (especially the Red Circle School stories), The Rover (starring rag-clad athlete Alf Tupper, the chip-chomping tough of the track, until he moved to The Victor in 1961), Eagle (with Dan Dare of the Inter-Planet Patrol, that most iconic of all comic characters) and The Topper (Beezer-sized and with Beryl the Peril and Mickey the Monkey), all of them swapped with schoolmates on a regular basis.

The girls at school didn't have to swap, they all got Bunty, which featured things like cut-out dolls with changes of paper clothing, puzzles and posters and The Four Marys, schoolgirls from somewhere that didn't really exist.

Everyone had a comic delivered and in the latter part of the 50s some of them, like The Dandy, were selling two million copies a week. Most cost 2d (now 16p).

A bit more grown up were war books, titles like Blackhawk, Fightin' Marines and Battlefield Action. The Germans, of course, were unceasingly portrayed as monsters of the very worst kind; the English were improbably good-looking, middle-class, immaculately mannered with a sense of fair play but with an understandable ruthless streak in order to save the world. And maybe add a bit on to the Empire while they were at it.

The enemy weren't actually called Germans, or even Nazis most of the time. Rather the Hun, Jerry, Krauts and Squareheads, all of them shouting non-stop. Usually a selection from Achtung! Donner und Blitzen! or Schnell! Schnell! And always getting obliterated by plucky English underdog heroes they referred to as Tommies, after the M1 Thompson sub-machine gun many of our brave boys carried.

The Japanese were Nips, yelling Banzai! at every opportunity, their Zero planes shot down almost at will by soldiers with puny handguns, their kamikaze pilots forever missing their target Allied ships and plunging into the depths of the Pacific to provide mealtime satisfaction for rampaging local sharks.

Away from comics, James Bigglesworth was rather more sophisticated, even if the end results of his wartime contribution were much the same. Lots of dead enemies.

Better-known to all boys as Biggles, the brainchild of Capt. WE Johns, he was a wartime pilot and adventurer to top the lot and his books really were legends in their own lifetime.

The first, The Camels Are Coming, published in 1932 (and about Sopwith Camel aircraft of course, not beasts of burden), set the tone for more than 150 books that were to follow:

> *"The Camel closed up until it was flying beside him; the pilot smiling.*
> *Biggles showed his teeth in what he imagined to be an answering smile.*
> *'You swine,' he breathed: 'you dirty, unutterable, murdering swine! I'm going to kill you if it's the last thing I do on earth.'"*

And of course he did. And of course it wasn't.

On a totally different plane, but no less fascinating to children, we all loved Enid Blyton.

The creator of Noddy, the Famous Five, the Secret Seven (and lots and lots more) was the one author no one could ignore, by far the most prolific writer of her era.

I wasn't too fussed about soppy little Noddy, although we all tried to draw him and Big Ears, but the Famous Five were so fantastic that Julian, Dick, Anne, Georgina (George) and Timmy the dog were known throughout the land for their thrilling adventures during holiday breaks from boarding school. There were 21 books in all.

I would read those stories in bed, secured with my borrower's card from Hemel Hempstead Junior Library. Lots of us signed up after we got a visit at school from one of the librarians. She was really nice and very encouraging, although she admitted she hadn't read all the books in the library. It wasn't quite clear what she did all day except stamp books.

But anyway it was free.

You could borrow two books a week, but had to pay a fine if they were late back. Even a day or two. So Mum made sure they weren't and got me different ones to read from a list of suggested books the librarian had given us, one for boys one for girls.

I read every night without fail, at first in the living room and then in bed, no matter how tired, no matter how cold. If not books, it would be comics and maybe even Luton Town football programmes given to Mum for me by a young girl whose mum she knew who went to every match, home and away. How wonderful that must have been.

Dad said reading was everything, it was vital, the source of all knowledge. We were so lucky, lots of the world weren't able to read and those who could read often couldn't afford to. I should read all I could at every opportunity.

Never in my life did I see him reading a book. Nor Mum.

Next to the fire there was a small dark brown bookcase, always open for the family to enjoy. That had nothing to do with potential easy access to the world of literature, but was entirely because the key was missing.

All it contained was a green and black Toby Jug that had been a wedding present (they didn't know who from), a couple of packs of cards, a boxed set of dominoes that rarely left its shelf, a shaky snowstorm plastic globe thing of Buckingham Palace and stacks and stacks of knitting patterns Mum used to swap with neighbours. No wonder all us kids looked the same.

The living room was the cosiest place imaginable. Unlike Benchleys Road, we had a brand new fitted carpet rather than the more accepted slippery combination of lino and a rug or two, like most people still had. Mum told everyone who would listen, meaning everyone because they couldn't avoid her words of wisdom.

On the carpet squatted a fashionably low three-piece suite covered in comfy thick cloth with flowers on, the settee bit facing the coal fire. In the grate stood Dad's pride and joy – a fireside set of long-handled brush and shovel and a poker, each of identical length and dangling around a central stand with a fancy carrying handle.

A true work of art he'd made himself out of brass and copper. Cost you a bomb in the shops, he reckoned. Quite rightly.

Dad explained to admirers who saw it that he sometimes had a few minutes to spare at work, particularly when he was on nights, and they often had bits of metal left over they didn't need. No point wasting it, it would only go out as worthless scrap. He'd brought it home to assemble it bit by bit over a few months since it was too heavy to carry in one go.

By the French windows was the table and four chairs we only really used for playing cards or board games, occasionally for a meal when real aunties and uncles came round. Like four or five times a year. The curtains at either end of the room matched the suite fabric up to a point.

The wall furthest from the door was dominated by the upright piano and its stool, but the sideboard facing it was the best bit, an Aladdin's Cave of toys.

I had a desk in my bedroom and plenty of space in my tallboy, but I never played up there. It was warmer than Benchleys, but still too cold, even in summer, not least because it never got the sun and there was only one small rug on the floor where I discarded my slippers and clambered in and out of bed.

So the sideboard became a toy cupboard, space for my favourites – in most cases the really special presents I got for Christmas. Plus the terrible Fuzzy-Felt Farm Animals.

This involved sticking the felt outline shapes of cows and pigs, fences and tractors and things on a gripping furry board to make a typical farmyard scene.

Except they didn't look anything like farm animals, they looked like felt outline shapes. There was no obvious scene, typical or not, and they certainly didn't stick on the board. And even if they had, what was the point? What do you do next, except take them off and stick them back on, maybe upside down or on top of each other?

I told Mum to chuck it out, but she said she couldn't because her sister had bought it for me specially and might ask to see it when they came round. She never did.

My microscope was in there, though, and that was more exciting than it sounds. I spent hours looking at strands of hair and carpet, bits of fingernail and various parts of flies, butterflies and wasps I'd killed then sliced with a kitchen knife when Mum wasn't looking. Blades of grass, flower petals, grains of salt and pepper. And bogies, lots of bogies. Everything literally took on a new look.

The fort was fun, too. It was nothing more complicated than a wooden square with high walls and walkways based on those erected by US soldiers within dangerous Indian territory. So realistic you could almost hear the bugle sounding Boots and Saddles, the signal to line up.

It even came with a plastic Stars and Stripes flag, which looked a little out of place since I only had plastic World War II Allied troops, tanks and guns and a few Japs called Tojo to defend the place. Not a US soldier in sight, let alone a covered wagon dashing for the safety of the fort gates or a ferocious war-painted Redskin scaling the compound with a knife between his teeth.

You could make your own fort and much else besides with a Meccano outfit and I had one of those tucked inside, too. It was outfit No. 7, I think, like the rest of the available range comprising mainly of lots of red and green metal strips and plates waiting to be held together by nuts and bolts and screws as you wielded a screwdriver and spanner in the hope of making something recognisable. A car, perhaps, maybe a crane, a plane or a boat.

It came with full instructions on how to create such things, but I wasn't much good at it. I tried to make the hull of a ship once, but Dad said it looked more like a slipper for a robot, which put me off a bit rather than encourage any possible career in mechanical engineering.

A big favourite was my John Bull Printing Outfit. Like Meccano, there were lots of them on the market, numbered according to the date of production and generosity of the box contents, but I think I had the No. 20 version.

You used tweezers to place small rubber reversed letters into a wooden rack to form words, pressed the completed message onto a spongy black ink pad, then stamped it on a sheet of paper. The outfits were so successful they became used in offices throughout the land, not just as toys.

The first stamp I made read Property of Steve and I stamped it on the cover of all my comics, just in case. And the door of my bedroom, although Mum wiped it off and made it clear it was not to re-appear. I stamped one on the inside of my wardrobe door instead and she never found that.

The John Bull and the rest were bit-players on the main play scene, though. Step up to the plate my all-time top toy, the second-hand Hornby Dublo electric train set.

Dad bought it for me one year off a bloke at work whose son was a bit older than me and had lost interest and his mum was always falling over it, she said. So I was presented with a huge cardboard box that had once been full of packets of soap powder and was now full of joy.

It lived upstairs in my bedroom with all the dozens and dozens of pieces of metal track inside it, but the key bits never left the sideboard.

There were two engines, one small black one I got out very rarely if only because it was a bit slow and anyway I had a real star, the envy of all my friends. A die-cast engine that was a model of the magnificent world-famous Kingfisher (number 60024), built at Doncaster Works in 1936.

With my trusty control box, I put it to work pulling either Pullman luxury passenger coaches or goods wagons emblazoned with their contents – Saxo Salt, Esso Royal Daylight Paraffin, Texaco Petrol, Lifebuoy Soap, Blue Circle Cement, Mobil, Oxo and Pickfords Removals.

In between them were anonymous closed containers carrying everything from furniture to horses and some open trucks, usually with lots and lots of bricks, aggregate, coal and coke.

There was always the tender behind the engine and a guard's van at the back. Every train had to have a guard's van and mine had an actual guard with a flag, peering down the track. How about that.

I had a station complete with stationmaster and a signal box just beyond it, inexplicably guarded by more plastic Japanese soldiers. And a level crossing, its gates usually closed to the stream of Dinky cars eagerly waiting to cross the track on their journeys to beneath the settee.

And what track! It was the original three-rail track made of tinplate, the middle rail being the source of the 12-volt current picked up by the locomotives. I had so much of it, straights and curves, left-hand and right-hand points, I could virtually fill the living room floor space, although Mum always seemed to need a bit for ironing or cleaning or something.

I curled it round from sideboard to piano and back again, with tracks going across as well, making tunnels under the chairs and in the middle of the room, using the playing cards from the bookcase.

They looked great until the door was opened and closed and the cards collapsed on the rails.

The inevitable huge impressive vase sat beneath the inevitable huge mirror on top of the sideboard, a colossus looking out almost challengingly towards the piano opposite where a smaller version resided, alone but for a huge metal ashtray with Player's written on it, which a kindly pub landlord had insisted on giving to Mum and putting it straight in her handbag.

All they lacked were flowers, a drawback in the vase world, I always thought. But then we never had cut flowers in the house. Flowers were for outdoors, said Dad. He never bought Mum flowers. Never. Never bought her a Valentine's card. Blimey, no. Didn't agree with it. How stupid to sign a card with a cross when it was obvious who it was from. Point made.

Every year she was disappointed because all her mates got one and showed them to her. But she never said, of course.

It was the same with Mother's Day. Not only was it a religious festival, and therefore to be treated with contempt, but (like Christmas and Easter) it had been hijacked by the wealthy conning the poor, as usual. Or something like that, I never grasped it fully.

Anyway, everyone knew the prices of bunches of flowers went up in the shops and they weren't even proper flowers, they were foreign. You could understand bananas and oranges because we can't grow them in England, but flowers? Disgusting.

At least Mum didn't have to spend any money on Dad for Father's Day. He was even more anti that. A contrived modern event, modern meaning since the Middle Ages, probably.

There were masses of wonderful flowers outside, though. Like Benchleys had been, the garden in Long Chaulden was always immaculate. Dahlias and gladioli remained favourites, lined up together like soldiers in a glorious bed down the left-hand side, staring across the lawn at the bank of roses opposite.

The combined ranks of multi-coloured annuals divided the lawn neatly into two, beyond which lived his vegetable plot, an expanse worthy of being opened to the public. Certainly more worthy of a better cook than Mum.

The whole garden was a masterpiece thanks to his pure hard graft, acquired knowledge and a meticulous attention to detail born out of being a precision engineer.

He even put iron filings around the roots of the hydrangea which dominated our front garden. Didn't like the blooms being pink, he explained, because they clashed with the colours of the other plants which formed guards of honour for the pathway. The iron will make them turn blue. And they did.

"Hard work never hurt anyone, son. You get out what you put in." That's what Granda said.

Granda knew everything in the whole world, although I never knew what he got out of being a postman.

14
Boys And Girls Come Out To Play

Boys didn't play with girls. They were a different breed. There was no obvious gender-led seating plan in the classroom, but there might as well have been. The boys talked to the nearest boys, the girls to the nearest girls.

They all had pigtails or bunches and smelt nicer than us. It wasn't as though we didn't like them, they were just, well, nothing like us...

We played football. Girls were into real rubbish stuff, like skipping about in the playground, two of them holding wooden handles at each end of a rope and twirling it round while lots more of them took it in turns to skip over the bit in the middle.

All they time they'd be chanting rhymes, like:

*"Nelly Murphy's got no drawers,
Will you kindly lend her yours,
'Cos she's going far away,
Ta Ra Boom De Ay."*

Tell me, please, what on earth is that about? Even worse:

*"1, 2, 3, my mother caught a flea,
She put it in the teapot and made a cup of tea.
The flea jumped out,
My mother gave a shout,
And in came a Bobby with his shirt hanging out."*

What's the point of all that? What's that got to do with somehow inspiring a better standard of skipping in the playground of Chaulden Junior School?

What's the point of hopscotch, come on? In a sentence, explain it. Or handstands up against a wall, your skirt tucked into your navy knickers while all the blood in your body suddenly starts sloshing around in your head?

By junior school, at least they'd got over plastic tea sets and pretending to make you a cup with imaginary milk and sugar (one lump or two, what boy would be that stupid?), but instead they had things like glove puppets. They had to.

Proper puppets, dangling from string attached to what looked like thin pieces of firewood, were far too difficult to operate and just ended in tangles, as we all saw when Jean brought one in which she'd been given for Christmas.

It was supposed to look like Mr Punch, but looked more like the bloke up the road who had a huge bulbous nose because he drank cider and his skin was really bad, said Mum, who often stared at his nose through the kitchen window.

So glove puppets it was, effectively large mittens in the form of Sooty and Sweep, Donald Duck and Tufty the Squirrel, which they could wave about while talking in silly voices. Especially when pretending to be the duck. Drove you mad.

Even sillier was a different version of hopelessly tangled string called a cat's cradle, a waste of time second to none. Basically, one girl tied string round her fingers, then transferred it by an ancient, established route to another girl's fingers. And back again. And again. That's it. Hours of young lives gone to pot.

Never did a boy have a go at that.

The only time boys ever got involved with tangled string on purpose was in conkers season, a glorious way of spending playtime in early autumn and making use of the otherwise useless fruits of the horse chestnut tree, which thrived in our part of the country.

We'd head off to the moorland by the A41 near the Swan pub (closed in 2010), just along from the grave of Robert Snooks, in 1802 the last highwayman in Britain to be hanged and buried at the scene of his crime, an £80 mail robbery, which equates to about £7,000 now.

Thousands are said to have flocked to the occasion, with Snooks, being driven by carriage through the latecomers, famously reassuring them: "No point hurrying, they can't start the fun until I get there."

Our crime was a touch less serious, if messy.

First, we vandalised the trees by chucking half-bricks at branches in order to fill our pockets with the shiny trophies-to-be, having extracted them from their fallen spiny casings. Back home, we used either a hammer and nail or a meat skewer to make a hole through the conker, then threaded through about a foot of garden string and knotted the end to hold it secure.

We were all tooled up ready to whack. Taking it in turns to strike, all you needed to do was smash an opponent's conker off its string and you had a winner. Do it again with the same conker and you had a two-er, a three-er and so on until your own champion was reduced to botanical rubble.

It was considered cheating to toughen the conker by soaking it in vinegar and getting your mum to bake it in the oven, which of course everyone did and everyone denied.

Boys just wanted to be outside, with other boys.

Scrumping apples from the nunnery in Green End Road was appropriately joyous. The St Mary's Dominican Convent, to give it full recognition, was a magnificent old manor house, which also had luxurious lawns and spectacular gardens.

A palace for the virtuous. Or, as Dad put it, a criminal waste of space.

Handily, though, its other boundary was an orchard which gave way to the woods on our side, by the allotments, where we'd sit up trees eating the nuns' fruit and sucking Oxo cubes someone had nicked from the grocer's in the village a few hundred yards away.

On the regular occasion of an irate sister or two emerging from within to point out the error of our ways, we'd send a volley of apple cores in their general direction. They'd shriek and make fists at us, then scurry back inside like so many demented penguins while we cackled like crows from the safety of our perches. It closed in 2004 because of a shortage of nuns.

Woodland also kept us safe at Boxmoor Golf Club, which closed seven years later, a beautiful expanse to one side of Box Lane, the road south to Bovingdon (a former RAF fighter station), where we had ample places to hide while engaged in the exciting if admittedly unlawful pursuit of members' golf balls.

We'd hear the thwack of club on ball from a distant tee, then pop out from our hiding places, secure the bouncing ball once it had come to a halt on the fairway and make a dash for it through the undergrowth long before they'd twigged what was going on.

The balls would subsequently find their way to a golf-playing bloke in Northridge Way (the only one we ever knew), who'd happily give us a few pence for our trouble. But best not to tell anyone about it, eh.

Knock Down Ginger was much more risky, but had the advantage of being legal if plain naughty. It was a game for two at the most, otherwise there was too much chance of getting caught.

All it involved was knocking on a door, always under cover of darkness just before we had to go home, then running off as fast as possible and hiding. The victim, carefully chosen for their obvious lack of athletic prowess, preferably old, fat or both, would come out, realise what had happened and look up and down the road, assuming we were long gone.

Ha ha, but that was the crunch. We were not long gone at all. We were only a few feet away, flat-down on the pavement the other side of their front garden bushes, our hearts pounding, pretending we were Commandos on some sort of nation-saving exercise which involved parachuting deep into occupied Chaulden then crawling on our bellies round a housing estate infested with murdering Krauts.

We all did it, except Peter. If his dad found out, he said, he'd get a strapping. His dad was always hitting him with the leather strap he kept on a hook inside the front door. His big sister used to get strapped, too, and everyone thought that was even more terrible. You never hit girls. Never. No matter what.

Everyone on the estate knew about it. No one talked to his parents. They were like lepers.

We were often up to more mischief just up the road, opposite the Tudor Rose, playing in air-raid shelters at the old National Camps Corporation site, which is now Pixies Hill Primary School. Oh, the irony – it was once a refuge for poor deprived children from London. You know, toe rags.

The shelters were scary places we'd enter through smashed-up doors with our torches on full beam, strewn with rubbish that we'd sift through, hoping to find examples of wartime activity. Tank shells, perhaps. A hand grenade or two would have been nice.

We never did, of course, and would just chuck things around instead, targeting the dilapidated buildings, breaking things for the sake of it because we knew the bulldozers would be there soon to flatten the fun.

Newer buildings could have been possible targets at Chaulden House Gardens. Once the site of an 19th Century country seat, now demolished, it was to be the latest chunk of the new Chaulden – originally scheduled to be finished by 1958 – with a large number of houses under construction, a stretch of them backing on to our gardens in Long Chaulden.

We could have got up to all sorts of mischief there, but were always being chased away by the navvies. And when it started to get dark they had security patrols with ferocious dogs. One of the dogs stared straight at me once and I froze with fright. Just like I always imagined would happen if I ever met The Woman Downstairs.

It was all too much for small boys. Besides which, we had to be indoors by then.

I had two modes of transport, one of them a Tri-ang scooter the bloke next door inexplicably gave me while I was chucking a tennis ball up the side of his house. I thought he was coming out to have yet another rant, since he usually worked nights and I was forever waking him up, but he just handed it over. Asked if it was any good to me.

Turns out it was just before they 'Did A Moonlight'. Mum explained that meant they'd been very bad people and hadn't paid their rent so they had to run away during the night when they couldn't be seen. They'd had to leave most of their stuff behind. Shame, she'd hoped she'd get some of it. No idea where they were going.

Granda said they'd done a flit, as in shit. Either way, we never saw them again and I got a bright red scooter. Perfect.

Even better were my Jacoskates roller skates which the teenage kid next door the other side gave me when his feet got too big. Didn't even want any money for them, which was decent. No one gave things away.

Worn with plimsolls and secured with red leather straps, they were forever slipping off, but were nevertheless handy for whizzing up behind the three-wheeled Express Dairy milk float and nicking the chocolate drinks off the back.

Mum wouldn't buy the drinks (waste of money), but sometimes stirred cocoa in a mug of cold milk for me, saying it was exactly the same, why pay more. It wasn't. It was disgusting.

The skates doubled as a kind of toboggan. Find a nice steep slope, place one fat chunk of wood (mine was a bit of next door's fencing acquired under the cover of darkness) on a single skate, sit down and away you go. After a few goes and an awful lot of grazes, it's surprisingly easy. If still potentially dangerous.

Zooming down the hill once, I nearly took out The Crippled Boy at the bottom as he came out from his gate on his crutches. I grasped some cotoneaster branches from the front garden of No. 5, enough to slow me down so I just missed him.

That could have been right nasty. He used to lean on his fence and watch us play football because he couldn't, what with his polio.

He got picked up by a small bus every day. A couple of other kids were already on it. We called it The Cripple Wagon. It took them to a special school. Don't know where. We never talked to him much or felt sorry for him. That's how it was.

"Always look out for people less fortunate than yourself. You never know when it might be your turn." That's what Granda said.

Granda knew everything in the whole world, although you assumed an ex-PoW had already had his turn.

15
Happy Parenting

The Hemel Hempstead dream for the Riches clan was working out nicely in the late 1950s. In the main, that is.

Dad still had the same secure factory job he'd once grasped with both hands, but which he had long since learned to loathe.

Loathed the routine, loathed having to stand at a machine for 48 hours a week – more when he could get much-needed overtime – with rests few and far between, precious time wasted by distrusting employers insisting workers clocked on and off even for a 20-minute meal break.

Loathed new advances in technology and the subsequent innovative machinery which reduced the skill factor of his job to zero when once he felt he was a tradesman.

Loathed the fact there could be no way out.

Loathed the lathe he once loved.

He was promoted just the once (in 40 years), joining the 'staff' as a charge hand. It changed his role only a little, although he never explained how. But it did mean he at last got paid for his annual summer holiday, which must have been a huge deal.

Mum told everyone he was now a foreman, virtually management, and could sack people. She was very happy about that. Granda said the unions wouldn't let him. Dad would never have sacked anyone anyway, even if he could. Which he clearly couldn't.

I was a bit confused.

Dad took it in his stride, as always. Life was what it was, he said, and he never wavered from that basic philosophy. No matter what. You make your bed and you lie in it. You only get the one chance, then you're dead. No coming back.

This was the opportunity he'd been given, to escape a far less privileged life in London. He'd gone for it and never, ever regretted it. He had no ambition other than looking after his family, which he always did to the very best of his ability.

Like every other kid, I thought my dad was the best dad in the world. Still do.

Like all the other mums in Chaulden, Mum had to go to work too, just as soon as Sally started at the infant school. But she was never going to qualify for the standard issue long-service carriage clock like Dad eventually did.

She was a waitress for a couple of years in a cafe in Bridge Street (now Hemel Cafe), which gave her the ideal hours of about 10 to 2, Monday to Friday. It was used almost exclusively by town centre office staff and shop workers from the nearby Timothy Whites, Woolworth's, Dolcis, Boots, WH Smith, Peter Percy, Bata, Dorothy Perkins, Radio Rentals, Cecil Gee, Mac Fisheries, Perrings furniture store, Burtons and a couple of others.

Plus the Big Five banks cosily tucked in together at the nearby Bank Court development – Midland, Lloyds, National Provincial, Barclays and Westminster.

Offices, unlike the factories out of the town centre on the industrial estate, hardly ever had their own canteens and shops very rarely sold sandwiches or hot drinks.

The cafe dished up bacon and eggs, homely pies, sandwiches, soup, omelettes, bangers and mash, that sort of thing. And fruit puddings or wedges of chocolate cake with custard or cream. Drinks were limited to tea or coffee, white or black, with or without sugar. It was modestly priced and packed every day with a hard core of regulars, but then it only had about 30 seats.

There was nowhere else to eat nearby apart from a truly grotty cafe next to the bus station toilets (the toilets had the edge on cleanliness), or just round the corner at Finlay's the tobacconist, which was more about tea and cakes than a proper meal and was full of really old smoke-smothered people with no clear destination left in their lives, disinterested in food, drooling over their drinks, hanging about waiting to die.

By pure coincidence, when Mum was a waitress we began having lots of meat pie, sausages and wedges of cake for tea, but she told us it was best not to tell people that in case we looked flash because she had such a good job and they probably didn't.

When the owners sold up and opened a new place in Watford High Street, Mum wouldn't travel the eight miles, even though they begged her, she said. Begged her. Not worth it, not the time taken, nor the bus fare to be paid.

Instead, she got a job on a school bus ferrying Catholics from all over town to the Blessed Cuthbert Mayne School on the Gadebridge estate. She really loved it, until she got the sack.

She told this kid off time and time again because he was the biggest on the bus and would bite the smaller kids just for a laugh. So eventually, and just as she had threatened, Mum dished out her version of justice, bit him on his arm and there was all hell to pay, said Dad, even though he was dead proud of her.

Anyway, the kid stopped biting others, so it worked in that respect, but Mum had to go when she was reported by the other mum.

Never mind. Her best-ever job followed – cashier at the smart new Sainsbury's store in the town centre. She loved it, especially the chance to natter away to all and sundry, eagerly soaking up any sort of gossip whatsoever from people she never knew.

Dad said he'd never get in her queue; you'd be there all day. Life was too short. Not that he ever went to a supermarket.

The hours and wages suited, the bus from home dropped her right outside the store in Marlowes and she could do all her shopping on a daily basis. But in reality she didn't. At break time, she preferred to sit in the tiny windowless tea room puffing away and nattering to the other girls through the fog, staying loyal to the Co-op up the road and the small shops of Boxmoor village.

Whatever job she did, she was always home before we were back from school and long before it was time to make tea.

We were never door-key kids at infant school age, nor were our friends. And when we were juniors, if any kid got home to a house and their parents were out, they just played in the street. Any problem, just knock on any door. We were all the same, after all.

If Mum got in early and it was summer she'd sunbathe in the back garden on her yellow striped deckchair with a nice cup of tea. Cups of tea were never anything other than nice. It wouldn't work: "Went next door today, had a really ordinary cup of tea."

Dad would moan if her deckchair left grooves in his lawn because she'd forgotten the long bits of slate he'd given her to put under the legs to stop that happening. He was rightly proud of his lawn. And everything that went on around it.

The whole garden was his. If ever a king had a council castle. Mum never lifted a finger out there, unless you count putting the washing out. Nor did he expect, nor want her to. It was always Dad's garden, even Mum called it that.

To even things up, it was always Mum's kitchen, cooking, washing, ironing, knitting and cleaning.

Dad always got off the bus at the stop over the road at 5.25pm, always the first off having always sat in the same seat at the front because the route started outside his factory gates. He knew all the drivers by name.

He always whistled across the road, skipped down the steps and unlocked the front door. Then unzipped his beige British Home Stores jacket, untied his Oxfords and placed them under the stairs, walked past the telephone table, which had presumably been purchased in anticipation of us actually getting a phone one day, and washed his hands in the kitchen sink.

The very second a cheek of his bum touched his seat – me on his left, Sally to his right – a mountainous plate of steaming-hot food was plonked in front of him on the grey Formica-topped table with drop-down leaves supported by swivel legs.

The evening mealtime view never altered. In pole position sat the pink china teapot covered with its keep-warm cosy, knitted by Mum from wool left over from various holiday jumpers.

Plus the two-pint yellow milk jug with an inch or two of liquid in the bottom, a green plastic tea strainer sitting in a dish and an industrial-sized sugar pot with 'sugar' emblazoned on the side, to avoid any possible confusion with its larder shelf companions 'flour' (always Spillers) and 'tea' (only Brooke Bond, loose).

Mum made full use of the Isle of Wight souvenir ashtray as she poured the tea, always in proper cups and saucers with spoons and always sugar first, then milk and tea. Often accompanied by yet another slating of those who challenged that established order. Like Aunty Laura. Sugar in last, apparently. Unbelievable.

Dad, meanwhile, attacked the delicious crusty split-tin loaf provided by Mansbridge Bakers of Cowper Road, Boxmoor, and handed us thick slices to smother in Anchor Butter on our side plates.

Mid-table hosted the Sarson's Malt Vinegar bottle and Heinz Tomato Ketchup, the rim always wiped post-meal with the dishcloth even if it hadn't been touched. To one side, the salt and pepper (always white, never saw black) jostled with the Lea & Perrins Worcestershire Sauce and Heinz Salad Cream, regardless of what was being served up.

Tea poured, bread cut, it was on to the table with the rest of the family's grub once Mum had put her fag out, sincerely apologising for the ash that had somehow found its way into the milk jug all by itself. Like last night and the night before.

The hot food was usually best. If she had a signature dish, it was oxtail stew. The tail boiled overnight, the thick fat lifted off from the surface in the morning when it had cooled, the meat torn in chunks, the bones discarded, then loads of carrots, onions and spuds piled in and reheated for an hour or two. Cooking didn't get any better than that.

No, really, not in this kitchen it didn't.

I loved Mr Brain's faggots, too, with big spoonfuls of tinned pease pudding. It looked like diarrhoea but was easier to spell, Granda said. I'd also give a thumbs-up for the fried beef sausages with onion gravy, but that's about your lot.

Otherwise, home meals were school dinners without the finesse, to put it nicely. She was more at home on that school bus biting people than in her kitchen.

Salad was particularly unimpressive, unforgivingly so since Dad managed to grow most of the very best freshest ingredients on his magnificent vegetable patch – the third of the No. 11 garden that was completely out of sight and out of mind to Mum.

No matter the imperious quality of the produce, it was hard to salivate over one tomato, unsliced, plonked on a plate with two leaves of cos lettuce, still dripping from their rinsing, a lone spring onion and a stick of celery while glaring at it all from the other side of the plate was a heap of tinned headless Glenryck pilchards awash with tomato sauce.

Worst of all was pigs' liver, fried in beef fat until it turned to dust. Or maybe the bullet-like lambs' kidneys, complete with inedible gristly bit.

But we knew nothing else and we ate everything. Even the slightest hesitation and we were reminded of starving children living in straw huts in Africa. It was miles away and scorching hot all the time. They couldn't grow things to eat and didn't have any money to buy them.

Everyone knew about them, there were posters in all the school corridors along with tons of things from the RSPCA, mainly ill-treated pet dogs with big eyes. Lots of people gave some money – to the RSPCA.

Afters was something like tinned peaches with evaporated milk or tinned mandarins with Bird's Custard, made from powder with boiling milk and stirred with a wooden spoon in a bowl in an ultimately futile attempt to get all the lumps out. Sometimes we'd have a sponge pudding or treacle tart instead, perhaps even chocolate mousse, always bought from the Co-op. With more custard.

The regular alternative was bread pudding, for some completely unknown reason a source of much satisfaction for Mum. It was rock cake, only rockier, a doomed coming together of stale bread, egg, raisins, cinnamon and who knows what else. Baked to oblivion. Then submerged in custard.

Mercifully, she never made much else from scratch, relying instead on shop-bought items like cheese and bacon pie, or tinned rissoles and Irish stew. All from the Co-op.

Dad said she was bloody hopeless when it came to cooking, but we didn't know much different. And how would he know anyway, since he didn't eat anywhere else? Even at work, in his break he had Mum's cheddar cheese and Branston pickle sandwiches. Every single day of his married working life.

"He's always liked them," she'd say.

"It's years too late to mention it now. I always swap them at work, have done for years. But don't tell her for chrissake," he'd say.

There was a time when we stopped having puddings altogether. Mum explained Dad was short of overtime at work, so we had to cut down a bit, but it didn't matter to Sally and me.

There was no question of anyone being hungry, because we just ate more bread and butter and there was always plenty of jam (mainly Robertson's apricot or raspberry) or treacle (Lyle's Golden Syrup, actually).

We weren't allowed to get down from the table until we were full up and we'd had our Haliborange tablet, which was good for you for some unknown reason. They tasted OK, all the kids had them.

And all that jam meant another collectors' delight – Golliwog badges.

The Robertson's jars all featured a friendly Golly with a black face, red lips and unruly hair, likened to American minstrel traditions and inspired by the company owner seeing small children playing with rag dolls on a personal tour of the US at the beginning of the 20th Century.

The jar labels came with tokens which you could collect and then send away for an enamel lapel badge. Everyone did, the badges were big news and we were forever swapping in an attempt to get the whole range – among them golfer (the first one, from 1928), bagpipe player, footballer, cricketer, jazz musicians, Scout, hockey player, ice skater, lollipop man and tennis player.

Some of the girls at school even wore a Golly pendant and chain. All the characters wore waistcoats with Golden Shred written on them, like the marmalade jars. More than 20 million were sent out before production stopped in 2001.

Bread and jam, even Mum's cooking, whatever it was, we just got it down us. There was never a mention of calories or carbohydrates, fat content or gluten, salt or sugar amounts. For the simple reason that we wouldn't have had a clue about any of them. No one did.

No one knew what a 'use by' date was, either. It hadn't yet been created by unscrupulous shopkeepers eager to suggest you throw perfectly good food away and then have to buy some more.

Everyone just did the sniff test. If it smelt off, you didn't eat it. If it had mould on it, you scraped it off, sniffed it and then ate it.

Food poisoning was completely unheard of, like vegetarians and food allergies or intolerances. No one came out in a rash or collapsed in a heap as a result of eating anything.

Always missing from the table, though, was anything remotely foreign. Or foreign muck, as Dad preferred to describe it. Garlic was just to hide the taste and it made you stink, curry disguised meat that was rotten, chillies made your bum sore and herbs (apart from his mint sauce) were just to tart up poncey food in big hotels so they could charge a fortune for it. Rice was for pudding. With jam.

Yep, Dad really hated foreign food. Not that he ever ate any.

In fact, Dad hated foreigners. Not that he ever met any. That's how it was.

Dad was all for the quiet life. He went to work, he came home. He had his tea, he went to bed. His hobbies were limited to gardening, fishing and decorating, the latter somewhat over-encouraged by his trouble and strife.

Not much else filled his life, apart from his trips to the pub two or three times a week.

He read the Daily Mirror, The People and the Angling Times, nothing else – although sometimes I found him flicking through my war books, perhaps thinking of what might have been.

Ending up like his own dad in a PoW camp? Killed, as a few of his slightly-older friends must surely have been? I never knew. And there was never any chance of him telling me, or me having the balls to ask.

Granda and Dad. The same emotional book briefly opened and just as quickly firmly closed. Like father, like son.

One of the high spots of Dad's entire life was the time he was actually pictured in Angling Times, or the Fishing Paper, as he always called it, cuddling a huge chub, which along with barbel were his coarse fish of choice and among the hardest to catch. He'd broken some record or other, I think for the size of the fish in that particular stretch of water.

He was so excited, an emotion which was anything but a regular visible occurrence. He went to the newsagent's and bought two more papers, one for Granda, one for the lads at work that he could leave hanging around the tea room. He knew they'd be really interested.

He told us how he'd caught the beast with his favourite rod, used a special-sized hook and had tempted it with either sweetcorn or luncheon meat. I forget which, but it sounded like a distinct step up from our normal tea, let alone fish fodder.

Dad was a star! Or a bit of one. I told all the boys at school, but they weren't much bothered, to be honest. It wasn't like it was football.

Mum didn't have any idea what a chub was. All she said was Dad had got his eyes closed in the photo, but she still tore out the page and put it in the sideboard drawer with all the birthday cards he'd sent her since the day they first met.

Dad even avoided reading the Local Rag, the Hemel Hempstead Gazette, which every house had delivered every week, although had he wanted to it would have been some effort to wrench it from Mum's hands.

All those lovely stories about all those dodgy people who'd ended up in the magistrates' court. May as well chuck the rest of the paper out, that's all she wanted apart from checking the list of dead people. Sometimes she knew the names of the defendants and would literally shriek out loud at the pages spread out in front of her on the draining board.

Hours of glorious true (for once) gossip for a few pence – especially when one of the blokes who came into her cafe was in there for nicking money from his cricket club. His ears must have been on fire for weeks.

She also took Woman's Own for stories about babies and film stars she'd never heard of, recipes she'd never attempt, a crossword she never finished and free knitting patterns.

"People get away with murder, but if you do so much as cycle on the pavement you end up in the paper and look a berk." That's what Granda said.

Granda knew everything in the whole world, although he didn't know anyone who'd been in the paper, like Mum did.

16

Money, Money, Money

The pudding issue was just part of a bigger problem for Mum and Dad, it turned out. A very much bigger problem.

One evening, when Sally had gone to bed and I was wrapped in my usual blue-striped Woolworth's pyjamas and bright red dressing gown, they sat me down on the settee in the living room and said they wanted to have a special talk.

They never did that. Not before, not afterwards. Special talk? What's all that? We talked all the time, no appointment necessary. What's going on?

Mum, standing up, had her hands clenched as tightly as her lips. Dad sat in his armchair, his head lowered as though suddenly fascinated by his own knees. For the first time, he addressed me as an adult. Telling me how it was.

They were up to their armpits in debt, that's how it was. I had no idea what the hell that meant, but whatever was going on I could reach out and touch the seriousness locked in that room that night.

I think they were genuinely frightened and it was really horrible for me.

Seems like they'd over-stretched themselves, been living beyond their means. And now they'd got a red letter from the electricity board threatening to cut off our supply. We'd have no lights, no cooker, no nothing.

I had absolutely no idea what I was supposed to say. But as luck would have it, I apparently had the solution.

What they needed to do was borrow some money out of my Post Office account to pay the bill and then everything would be all right. They would pay the money back to me as soon as possible. Every week, they'd put in a regular amount and show it to me.

They needed £20 (I think it was 1959, so equivalent to about £427 in 2018). All I had to do was sign the appropriate part of my Post Office Savings Bank Book. They explained it was a record of money contributed by both sets of grandparents and assorted other relatives when they didn't have a clue what to buy me for Christmas and birthdays when I was very small.

Since Premium Bonds came out in 1956, they'd taken to buying me those instead. Not only were they an investment for the future, there was a chance of winning money, like the football pools. I'd seen some of those, somewhere around the house.

But I had absolutely no idea what a Savings Bank Book was, let alone any idea I had one, until Mum tearfully produced it from the top drawer of the sideboard.

It was the first thing I ever signed.

Some of the financial over-stretching was blamed on the new General Electric fridge. Hardly anyone else had one of those (only 34 per cent of the country to be precise), Mum would say proudly, pointing out that the milk was much colder than it had ever been in the larder and we could make ice cubes in a special little tray at the top.

Dad was of the opinion that more people were likely to stick their heads up a polar bear's arse than plug an ice box into the mains electricity supply.

But Mum pressured him on the idea of keeping his home-grown veg fresh for longer and not running the risk of meat going off in hot weather, not like that nice joint of lamb had done last summer. All those maggots all round the larder. The ugliest wriggling mass you'll ever see. Had to throw everything out. You can't be too careful.

Sold.

He never ever took it upon himself to create an ice cube, mind.

More dosh went on Mum's (no household goods were ever a man's issue) very latest model vacuum cleaner, a Hoover Junior. Brilliant, much better than the old one Nanna had given her. Might as well chuck out the dustpan and brush. The place will be far cleaner than it's ever been. Amazing how much dust these things can suck up.

Sold.

Oh, and the Hotpoint Twin Tub washing machine. There were adverts for it all over the place. Anyone who was anyone was getting one, or something like that. Even that couple over the road who've never got two ha'pennies to rub together, they've got one.

Sold.

At least my electric train set didn't get a mention, although it had done some months earlier when they were looking to cut back on the juice. Just before that letter from the electricity people probably.

The twin tub got her most excited, but it was hardly a complete energy-saver in either the physical or power supply sense.

The washing machine side had to be filled with hot water via a rubber tube attached to the tap. Then, when the clothes had magically whizzed about and washed themselves with the aid of Tide powder, Mum had to haul them out with tongs and place them in the spin drier half of the contraption, assuming she could see it through the cloud of steam that had engulfed the entire kitchen.

Then it was back to emptying the washing side, refilling with water, and rinsing the contents of the spin drier when that had finished. Then drying again. They may even need a further rinse. And you had to do it all with whites and coloureds separated, of course. And the items always got tangled up.

On completion, the whole load was shared around the warmest parts of the house to dry fully. Reminded him of a Chinese laundry, said Dad, who'd never felt the need to visit one.

He was aware, though, that each of Mum's new luxury items had one thing in common. She didn't yet own any of them. They all came on the never-never.

More accurately called Hire Purchase (HP), it was a means of the masses getting their hands on goods they couldn't afford at the time. Rather than save for an item and then buy it, they could pay a deposit of up to, say 25 per cent, get their hands on the goods, then pay off the rest (plus quite a lot extra) on a weekly basis over a period of months.

Everyone we knew bought things that way, just as everyone now has a credit card or signs a car leasing deal. And the minute something was getting close to being fully paid for, another item would be ordered.

So the very people who were least likely to have the cash to buy expensive goods were the ones most tempted and the most likely to be surrounded by them – and therefore permanently in debt.

What would be next? The TV was top of the wish-list, but they were too dear. Perhaps when Dad gets his next pay rise we can get one from Radio Rentals and pay week by week. Lots of people were doing that, like Aunty Laura.

And anyway we needed a new three-piece suite because those people we'd met at the holiday camp were coming to visit us from Birmingham as soon as they could make it.

Mum was just waiting for the promised letter. She'd been waiting months, but they were probably very busy, living in such a big place. Such nice people, apart from the girl.

The post-mealtime chats were dominated by romantic reviews of the past along with extravagant dreams of the future, none of which would ever happen. The present took a back seat.

Us kids were never encouraged to talk about school, Dad certainly went out of his way to avoid any mention of work and wasn't keen when Mum went on and on about her job.

You couldn't blame him. I mean, who cared that Mr Cardigan from the bike shop wanted horseradish with his ham and tomato toastie today when only yesterday he'd gone for cheese and onion and Daddies Sauce?

The past loomed large, though, and I loved it. Loved hearing about those Olden Days when things cost virtually nothing, when everyone looked after everyone else and families stuck together. Those were the days. There was nothing bad to report.

Well, apart from a couple of world wars, a life expectancy of 48 when Granda was born, rampant diseases, inadequate schooling, transport, clothing and health care, slum living, malnutrition, endless strikes, ever-increasing violence and crime, mass unemployment and general abject poverty.

Every night we chatted, except Fridays. That was when Dad opened his brown paper wage packet with the neat holes punched in it, tipped the contents on the table and pushed the housekeeping money for the coming week towards Mum, who immediately counted it.

The rest, and that didn't amount to much, he slid into the left-hand pocket of his trousers, almost guiltily. Beer money.

Then he produced a book from out of the table drawer and wrote things in columns. I didn't know what at the time, but he was comparing everything to last year.

So Sally and I got out of the way once we'd eaten our fish and chips since it was clearly none of our business.

"Money is the root of all evil." That's what Granda said.
Granda knew everything in the whole world, although he'd never had any money.

17
Politics And Religion

In 1959, Mum caught a serious dose of religion, which threatened the stability of 11 Long Chaulden.

A new church, St Stephen's, just up the road and opposite the pub, opened its doors and released the charismatic young bachelor vicar, Rev Ian Graham-Orlebar, who toured the estate on his motorbike wowing the locals (mainly women) with his decidedly unstuffy, not normally accepted church-like, views.

He was fat. He was bald. He spoke posh. No matter. Mum was impressed enough to go to a couple of services and before you could say JESUS CHRIST! (as Dad began to, far more frequently) she was flower arranging and helping clean the adjoining church hall.

In the main, this involved getting the sick off the floors and walls the day after one of Ian's new 'The Church Needs Youth' evenings, which attracted some of God's least well-chosen people with access to underage liquid refreshment and a record player, which hardly anyone had at home, capable of blasting out the works of Buddy Holly, Billy Fury, Tommy Steele, Neil Sedaka, the Everly Brothers and everyone's overall favourite, a certain Elvis Presley.

Dad's reaction bore none of the hallmarks of religious tolerance. He simply thought she'd gone round the twist.

Especially the night she wanted us all to say grace before she poured the cups of tea which heralded the start of the evening meal. That was never going to happen, although she did bow her head a bit as Dad sliced the bread.

And Dad was unusually close to getting very cross when the words 'Sunday school' were casually introduced into a teatime conversation. For the first and only time.

He didn't even like the fact that a Scout troop had been formed at the new church, the 3rd Chaulden Sea Scouts, who wore uniforms akin to sailors, complete with impractical hats and lanyards.

Hemel was about as far from the sea as you can get in England, more than 50 miles, so the idea was obviously stupid. He hoped they wouldn't mess about down by the canal and disturb the fish.

Even worse, should I be tempted to think of joining their Cubs pack

I'd have to become a regular churchgoer. He knew that was part of the deal. Neither of us fancied that.

And anyway, said Dad, they'd only put up the Church of England building in the first place as competition for the begging bowl (donations) because 200 yards further up the hill, past the shops and the Rent Office (now a chemist), was the much larger Methodist St George's Church, who ran a Boys' Brigade company rather than Scouts. Same horse, different jockey.

Scouts' aim: To do their duty to God and the Queen.

Brigade aim: The advancement of Christ's kingdom among boys.

Right load of weirdos they all were, he reckoned. An opinion clearly not open to any debate.

Frustrated at Dad's blindingly obvious lack of religious fervour, Mum must have gone to work behind the scenes because one night there was a knock at the door and, would you Adam and Eve it, there stood Ian in his jeans and plimsolls. He'd come for a chat. With Dad.

Ian, left on the doorstep like all callers, rain or shine, expressed his disappointment that he hadn't ever seen Dad in church. Dad told him that unless he was very much mistaken he hadn't seen the vicar in the Tudor Rose on darts night.

And so it came to pass... the very next Friday, Ian turned up in the pub with his own darts in his top pocket and apparently gave as good as he got, both on the board and in the beer-drinking stakes.

That impressed Dad (and his mates), I know it did, but he still wasn't for turning.

I never knew Dad change his opinion about anything at all, even the most trivial of things, and he wasn't about to start now just because of a posh bloke with his collar on back to front, as he liked to put it.

Dad hated religion with a passion. Any religion, there was absolutely no prejudice on his behalf. God bothering, he always called it. He was the complete non-believer, fond of pointing out to those of faith how he regularly got beaten by those Roman Catholic nuns as a schoolboy. In any other walk of life they would have been locked up, he maintained.

He reserved a special loathing for the Sally (Salvation) Army, whose local band played at the junction of Long Chaulden and Northridge Way most Sunday mornings and who had their headquarters in town, near the bus station in Waterhouse Street.

The music wasn't the problem, in fact they belted out a damn good Onward Christian Soldiers, he happily conceded, it was all about the tin rattling. Rattled by the same people who thought drinking was a social crime, yet routinely went begging in pubs to fund whatever it was they did, most particularly the Tudor Rose on Friday nights when he was playing darts and didn't welcome any intrusion. Bloody hypocrites.

Most of all, though, he hated the change in Mum. He didn't really like any change.

I noticed it once in particular when I got home from school to find Mum all hot and bothered. She'd got back on a bus from town so crowded that the conductor hadn't got round to her. She therefore had no option but to get off without paying for a ticket.

Before, she would have considered it a stroke of good fortune. Now, horror of horrors. Thou shalt not steal, and all that.

I was duly sent off with her fare on the two-mile return walk to Two Waters Bus Garage (demolished in 1995), where I explained what had happened to a bemused uniformed man who sat behind a grubby desk in the office by the main gate, below the staff snooker room.

He told to me to keep the money, but I explained I couldn't because my mum was very religious. So he took it off me and put it in a drawer. When I got back Mum asked where the ticket was, but I hadn't been given one. So she was still worried, but I wasn't allowed to tell Dad in case he thought she was being stupid.

Fortunately, the new Mum didn't last more than a year or so. The religion bug left her as fast as it had struck when a favourite old real aunty of hers died after a long and painful illness and she couldn't understand why God hadn't spared such a lovely woman despite all her praying.

Dad calmly pointed out that Mum could hardly expect her god to prevent the death of all of us on the planet, no matter how nice we were. There wasn't enough room, for a start.

I have no idea the effect that little speech had, but she never went to church again. Didn't even let us go banging on neighbours' doors while carol singing, which was a shame. We always got a few bob doing that, starting the minute the calendar flipped over to December.

Suddenly, she thought it was nothing more than shameless begging for money from people on the estate who couldn't really afford it.

For a short time, it had been tunefully spreading the word of God.

Mum was even keener on local politics, dragging us kids around early evenings as she canvassed for the Labour Party at various elections. Any old election would do. This time, Dad fully endorsed it as a paid-up party member, although he never took anything like such an active role.

She'd jump on the bus and go to Labour Party meetings all over the various Hemel estates. No community centre escaped her attention and local councillors would come to the house. She'd make endless cups of tea and play the Red Flag on the piano.

At election times, she went door knocking every night during the build-up, asking those who answered the call whether the party could count on their vote. The best trick was to get a Labour supporter who had a car to promise to collect would-be supporters and take them to the polling station.

Mum assumed everyone who had a car would vote Tory, but then hardly anyone on our estate had one. All over Chaulden, the front windows had red posters in them with poorly-printed pictures of the candidates. Never saw a blue one.

Her activities in that respect earned a pat on the back from another fully paid-up Labour Party member.

"Tories? Scum. Beware of them. Do the likes of us nothing but harm." That's what Granda said.

Granda knew everything in the whole world, although he could be a bit blinkered when it came to politics.

18
Starting Work

I was 10 years old when I started work. Not up a chimney or in a gang out thieving, like Granda told me they used to in the Olden Days (not him, though). No, just along the road. All the boys got Weekly Errands as soon as they reached 10. The girls didn't. Happy birthday, son, here's the shopping bag.

Armed only with a light-brown, but enormous, hessian bag containing a small and empty Sarson's Malt Vinegar bottle and a plastic-beaded (half missing) purse crammed with assorted coins, a couple of notes and a shopping list, I was pointed in the direction of St John's Road, the main route through Boxmoor village, every Saturday morning without fail, or any consideration of the prevailing weather.

Mum was reluctant to use the Chaulden estate shops only 300 yards up the road, or liked me going there, because of all the kids hanging about getting in the way and causing mischief. Toe rags, she called them. Ahem.

There were two exceptions, most notably and appropriately Barker's newsagents because of her fags. By now she was coughing up Kensitas (every morning it was like having a barker of a dog), mainly because the packets of 20 contained gift tokens.

Collect enough of them to set you on the way to lung cancer and you might get a set of Working Shire Horses place mats as pre-terminal compensation.

She also continued to use the Co-op for essential items, largely food she was unable or unwilling to cook. Plus scratchy Izal Medicated toilet paper, which handily doubled as tracing paper, Tide washing powder, Flash floor cleaner, Dreft washing-up liquid, Vim sink cleaner and Windolene. All because of her divi.

The ubiquitous dividend, that is, ostensibly shared by Co-op members nationwide. It's your shop, in you go, spend your money, share the proceeds. Utopia of the tills. The ultimate 1950s store loyalty card.

You kept a book of what you spent, retained receipts to prove it, then got a twice-yearly cash handout according to your expenditure. Every mum had her own personal divi number and they never forgot it, rather like the men who had wartime service numbers, but with rather less danger involved.

She drew the line at Green Shield Stamps, though, reels of which first arrived alongside British tills from 1958. They were given away by lots of petrol stations and stores, notably Tesco, according to the amount spent.

You stuck them in savings books and then exchanged the books for gifts from a catalogue. You needed a wheelbarrow-load to get something as life-changing as a plastic photo frame or a dartboard.

She couldn't be bothered with all that, though Dad thought a dartboard might sit nicely alongside the living room mirror if they moved that years-old blurred photo of dead Uncle Chas out of the way.

I hated going shopping with Mum. We always met some boring woman with a child in tow and they'd make us stand back to back to see who was tallest, which was usually me. So what? What was the point of that?

Then they'd stand in the middle of the pavement, seemingly selecting a portion that was most in the way of other people, and go on and on about neighbours, babies and prices. Hardly ever anything else. There were regular attempts to draw us into conversation, a deliberate ploy in the hope of wasting more time.

"Blah, blah, blah, didn't we, Steve?" Stock reply: "Yes, Mum."

"Blah, blah, blah, don't you think, Steve?" Stock reply: "Yes, Mum."

And so on, for what seemed like hours.

I mentioned this to Granda once and he was very helpful. He said women always talked shit.

My Boxmoor shopping route began at the furthest point, half a mile from home, with the baker's. Four white-iced buns to the good, destined to be packed with marmalade on my return, it was then back along the road to Charman's Butchers, where I joined the queue which snaked outside way beyond the chemist's next door, then took my turn to hand over the list from Mum detailing her required size/price of various items.

Take your pick from scrag end of lamb, faggots, beef sausages, Sunday beef joint, oxtail, chops, mince, kidneys and liver. She would write a note at the bottom, something like: "If the chops are any dearer this week than last, we'll have more mince, please. Thanks, J. Riches."

The butcher, resplendent in his beefy brown and white striped apron, would weigh then wrap all the meat individually in thick white paper. Then he stacked the packages into a large brown paper bag, on the side of which he'd scrawl all the prices using the pencil tucked behind his ear.

You then had to take the bag to a large stone-faced old woman wedged in a small box in the corner of the tiny shop for her to turn all those figures into a bill, slap it down in front of you and reach out for your money, never letting a word escape from her clam-like lips.

If your shoes were wet when you entered the shop, by the time you went back outside you were coated with sawdust halfway up your shins. If they'd been dry, the sawdust would instead have infiltrated them, rendering the shoes half a size too small.

Next stop, the greengrocer over the road next to Lloyd's Bank. Another queue, but no list required, the same things every week. First, get the Sarson's bottle filled with malt vinegar from the barrel on the counter. Help yourself, Sonny.

I was called that a lot. And Sunshine. Men got called Squire, Chief, Cock, or John. Which was often handy for Dad, being a genuine John.

Then, seasonally-selected white or red spuds weighed and tipped straight from the bowl of the scales into the shopping bag, carefully by-passing the bag of meat and the buns on the way down, soon followed by carrots and greens. Whatever greens they had – cabbage almost always.

On to the draper's. Obviously, no one could afford to buy all the wool for a self-knit jumper in one go, so mums like mine chose their wool after studying knitting patterns, then put their name to a whole bag of the stuff (with its special colour batch number) to be reserved at the shop, buying one-ounce balls as they could afford them. Weekly.

I queued up and handed over Mum's order card and cash and the old lady ticked one of the remaining boxes before grabbing a stepladder so she could fetch the wool from one of the many bags neatly aligned on the packed shelf above her. The times I saw her go up and down that ladder. It was a right rigmarole, couldn't she just put them somewhere at ground level?

The turn of the grocer, but only to get bacon for Sunday morning breakfast. Mum got the other groceries from the Co-op, but their bacon wasn't as good, apparently. Half a pound of green streaky, please. Never smoked. We'd had enough of smoke back in Harlesden, said Dad.

Occasionally, there was an extra stop to make – for my three-monthly economy haircut, which Granda reckoned helped lessen wind resistance and gave me a head start at sport. Barry Austin, the Boxmoor barber trained by his father George, and who remains in business there, had two styles: short back and sides, or the rather more popular very short back and sides.

He had a black and white brochure in his shop by the bus stop that you could flick through while you waited (it always seemed ages) and pick a fashionable style. You may want to look like James Stewart, say, Kirk Douglas, or even Norman Wisdom, for a laugh. Whatever look you fancied, it became a Barry special. We all looked exactly the same.

And finally, home. But only after the scariest stop of the lot. The last shop in the village, a general store opposite the doctor's, was the tiniest but loudest – from the bell that automatically rang when you pushed the door open, to the radio blaring out from the back room.

The owner emerged through the multi-coloured plastic blinds with a deep and curt "Morning" that appeared to come from her boots. Yes, laced-up boots. And dark clothes, a red scarf and cropped hair. A visual rival to everything I imagined about The Woman Downstairs.

I always took two bundles of firewood from a coffin-like wooden box near the door, gave her the money and got out as fast as I could. During the fire-free warmer months, I would scurry past the shop on the other side of the road, never looking across.

I told myself to grow up, don't be stupid. But I couldn't help it.

The whole Saturday shop didn't take too long, but sometimes the bag was really heavy and it was a bit of a struggle. I had to keep changing hands every few yards. I never mentioned it, didn't want to look like a girl.

The best of the weekly errands came every Friday night, going down to the Westons chippy in the village.

Sid the Fish was behind the stainless-steel jump, a ginger-topped and freckle-faced jolly man with haddock-like flesh which clearly had seen no more daylight than the flour-dusted occupants of the wet marble slab alongside him.

Sid would dole out the most amazing fat and soggy half-charred chips to go with our rock salmon entombed in dark brown batter and a bit of skate for Dad, who ate all the bones – rather like he ate apple cores, thick cheese rind and the stalks of Brussels sprouts.

Sid ensured I got it all home while still warm by wrapping it in so many pages of the Gazette (out the same day) it was like carrying a small child. The smell was fantastic and the joy of wolfing it down, showered with vinegar, dusted in salt and accompanied by bread and butter and a glass of milk chilled in our fridge, lives on for ever.

For doing the Weekly Errands, I got two bob (2s/10p, now £2.10) a week.

"Never be out of work, son. There's always a job for someone somewhere, just that lazy buggers can't be bothered to look." That's what Granda said.

Granda knew everything in the whole world, although he was lucky to have a job for life.

19
Football Crazy

Away from the classroom, nothing beat football. Football all the time. No one could get enough football.

How I loved my football boots, the ultimate in hand-me-downs from Dad, which he'd had when he was a kid. The leather was tough and wrinkled like an Eskimo's face (we'd done them at school), the yellowing nails from the studs regularly invaded the soles, the interior stuffed with torn rag so they came at least some way to fitting me a lot more than 20 years after their purchase.

He polished them for me with Chelsea Royal Boot Dubbin and I wore them with pride on regular excursions with the other boys to the vast field alongside Chaulden Lane, which followed the original line of the old Roman road Akeman Street, the cross-England link between Watling Street and the Fosse Way.

The whole area was officially called Chaulden Lane Playing Field. But we always called it Down The Field. Everyone knew where that was.

It was home to Camelot Rugby Club, who had a clubhouse one end, a mysterious bunch of sportsmen whose pursuit was entirely unknown to us. Particularly when they came out wearing what looked like football kit, but with some of them wearing hats. When they played, with a different ball, they threw it and grunted a lot. We had no idea what they were doing.

The rest of the field space was ours, often just Phil and me, and we spent a huge chunk of our lives down there, tearing around with our FA approved-weight footballs, taking it in turns to take on the 'keeper role between the posts of the giant goals that stood at each end of the three enormous pitches.

Saturday mornings were best, when Patrick the council groundsman dragged the goal nets from his hut near the swings and draped them around the framework, secured with tent pegs. We then had a good couple of hours of whacking the balls in there, thrilled at the unique sound of ball hitting net and rolling towards the back. Delighted, too, that we didn't have far to go to fetch the ball and resume the action.

And then the men of Chaulden United would arrive for a West Herts League match. We stood behind the home goalkeeper as they went about their opponents, perhaps Northchurch or Chipperfield, dreaming that one day we could pull on the black-and-white shirt, like the bloke next-door-but-one did.

Even though he was too fat and too slow, according to Dad. Who of course never saw him play. And who was a lot fatter and a lot slower, let's be honest here. Dad's weight scarcely altered from the 14st mark, which was quite enough to carry if you were only 5ft 9ins, an inch shorter than Mum.

Whether watching or playing, there was always a rush to get back for Saturday evening radio, starting with Sports Report with the football results at 5pm, then Top of the Form at 7.30pm.

They were both to prove hugely significant, Top of the Form because I loathed getting the answers wrong, which was all the time since it was a nationwide quiz contest for secondary schools featuring kids of varying ages, 13-18. As I got older, I'd write down all the questions and memorise all the answers, jealous of their knowledge.

But Sports Report, introduced by Eamonn Andrews, was my No. 1 show ever. If anything cemented my early love of football, it was this. The results (read by John Webster) themselves were pure fascination, but looking behind the scenes at the statistics and facts surrounding the clubs became almost an obsession. Well, not so much of the almost.

Time and again I'd sit at the living room table and write down all the Football League teams in alphabetical order, plus the divisions they played in, the names of their grounds, nicknames, colours, trophies won, record attendances etc., etc.

I knew most of the details of all 92 clubs in the entire Football League, no problem. A mate knew all the First Division phone numbers, too, even though no one had a phone. We thought he was a genius because nerd wasn't a word in circulation at the time.

I was only eight when the 1959 FA Cup Final kicked off (on Saturday, May 2, 3pm), but I can still name both teams.

Luton Town: Baynham, McNally, Hawkes, Groves, Owen, Pacey, Bingham, Brown, Morton, Cummins, Gregory.

Nottingham Forest: Thomson, Whare, McDonald, Whitefoot, McKinley, Burkitt, Dwight, Quigley, Wilson, Gray, Imlach.

Forest won 2-1, despite Roy Dwight breaking his leg after half an hour, meaning they played the rest of the game with only 10 men, substitutes not being allowed until 1965. They deserved it, everyone said, but it was a pity in one way because I really wanted Luton to win

137

since they were so close to Hemel, even though I'd never been there.

It had a special significance in being the first game I ever saw on TV (at Steve's house, we had no telly until I was 12, the phone followed a year later) and one of the highlights of my whole life, not merely a big day for an eight-year-old.

I'll never forget hearing 100,000 people singing football's adopted hymn Abide With Me (sung to the tune Eventide), and later the Nottingham fans chanting Robin Hood, Robin Hood, as they regularly did at their home games. It was such a huge, huge event. There was nothing like it in the world, nothing.

Aunty Laura made us plates of paste sandwiches while we watched the match with Steve's dad, Frank, and the women sat in the kitchen, smoked loads of fags and talked about the woman over the road whose husband had got banged up after a fight in the pub at the bottom of the High Street which Dad and his mates always referred to as the Bucket of Blood.

When I got home I started reading my favourite book all over again, the first autobiography I ever read – Tommy Lawton's Football Is My Business, published in 1947. I struggled with many of the words, but it didn't put me off and there were some great photos in the middle.

Lawton was the greatest centre-forward ever, reckoned both Granda and Dad. He played for Burnley at 16, was sold to Everton as Dixie Dean's replacement when he was 17 and was in the England team at 19.

He came from the poorest of backgrounds, was as hard as nails and smashed goalscoring records wherever he went. Had his career not been interrupted by the war, he may well have set records that would never be beaten.

I was never going to be a Lawton, but at 10, and by now the proud owner of new boots that didn't actually hurt me, I played my first competitive football match for Chaulden Juniors. We all piled on a little coach one afternoon already wearing our short-sleeved V-necked blue shirts and black shorts.

Off we went across town to Chambersbury Primary School, on the Bennetts End estate, and lined up in the traditional 2-3-5 formation with me at left half, the customary fat kid in goal, two slightly less fat kids as full backs and a couple of little whippets as wingers.

We won 2-0, I think, much helped by having Dave at centre half, a position he later occupied with much distinction for Fulham, Cardiff City and Wales.

We never wanted the football season to end, but it did promptly at Easter. Then cricket took over and I loved that, too. Like all the other schools nationwide, we had all the gear, proper bats and balls, stumps and bails, gloves and pads and a well-mown grass strip.

Mr Perfect (yes, really) was the teacher in charge as we took to the field with everyone wanting to bat like Ted Dexter or Colin Cowdrey, and bowl like Fred Trueman or Brian Statham. But the closest I got to glory was hitting the headmaster with the ball during a match we played on a school open day. He clapped in my direction because the parents were watching, but everyone knew he was livid and his shin must have been throbbing.

Tennis was only for posh people, so the nearest I got to that was dribbling a tennis ball all the way to school, left foot up the road, then right foot all the way back on the other side. I was told every day to remember to pick it up to cross the main road, but of course never did.

Even when I wasn't actually playing, my sporting interest wasn't entirely restricted to football. The only time our kitchen radio dial turned towards the highbrow Third Programme was when ball-by-ball cricket commentary was provided by Test Match Special.

How I loved the tones of John Arlott and co, whether in England at Lord's or elsewhere, or telling us all about our gallant boys in white in Australia, South Africa or, most romantic of all, the West Indies.

I read Dad's Daily Mirror over breakfast every day and not a word of the sports pages was missed, even if it involved tennis and tales of Rod Laver when I'd never seen a game of tennis in my life. I followed the exploits of Maria Bueno, too, but only because it looked like Maria Beano.

Oddly enough, I always started the paper by looking at the Andy Capp cartoon. It was never very funny; I was only interested because Flo was just like the woman in the butcher's.

Then it was on to sports writers like the peerless Peter Wilson and whatever he was on about. Every event, big or small, I read about it. I learnt just as much about reading and writing at the kitchen and dining room tables as I did at school.

But my very first Olympics, the 1960 Games in Rome, stands out in my memory most, especially the exploits of Abebe Bikila of Ethiopia, who won the marathon running with no shoes. Jesus. Ran 26 miles. No shoes. Jesus again. Beat the best in the whole world.

And Cassius Clay, of course, the light-heavyweight upstart who won boxing gold for America. A mouthy Negro, they were saying over there in the States. The Louisville Lip. He'll soon get his comeuppance. Dad said he had the fastest hands ever, but even if he stepped up to heavyweight he'd never be as good as Joe Louis.

Joe was Dad's all-time hero. Shaded it from Lawton, Denis Compton and Endless Gossip, who won the Greyhound Derby at White City in 1952. He'd had his picture taken with one of them – yes, the dog. It was in a drawer up in the bedroom.

And the big disappointment of 1960? Everyone said Brian Phelps, even though he was only 16, would get a gold medal for us in the diving, but he only came third. Mind you, not many people except me really cared about diving, I suppose.

Great Britain got just two gold medals – Anita Lonsbrough in the 200m breaststroke, where she broke the world record, and Don Thompson in the 50k walk. I didn't even know there was such a sport. We only got 20 medals in all and finished 12th behind little countries where hardly anyone lives, like Romania and Australia.

The Daily Mirror said it was a terrible performance. Granda said we were shit.

The first big football match I ever went to was the 1961 FA Amateur Cup final between Walthamstow Avenue and West Auckland Town at the Empire Stadium, Wembley, on April 22 (3pm).

Dad, Granda and me walked the three miles from Springwell Avenue to the stadium and set about cheering on the Londoners against a side from who-knows-where (Co. Durham, revealed Granda, although that didn't really help much).

Match memories are vague, mainly because I was too little to see everything properly from our seats, but I know Avenue's monster of a front man, Jim Lewis, stood out and it was he who got the winning goal in a 2-1 result in front of a 45,000 crowd. The noise was incredible, the first time I got that amazing goose-pimple feeling you only ever get at football matches.

I was able to tell Dad and Granda that both Lewis and the Avenue captain, Stan Prince, had played in the 1956 Great Britain team in the Melbourne Olympics, where they were beaten 6-1 by Bulgaria. I'd read it in Charles Buchan's Football Monthly in the barber's. They didn't seem to care much.

At half time Granda bought me a foot-long hot dog called a Doodledog, which came smeared with sweet brown mustard in a limp and dry bread roll that was so much smaller you had to bite the ends off the sausage before they fell on the ground. One of the best things I'd ever eaten.

My overriding memory of that great day? I wasn't allowed a second one. Kids, eh.

We came back to Jubilee Clock on the Route 662 trolleybus via Stonebridge Park and Craven Park, its red exterior as always plastered with adverts for Exide Batteries and Ilford camera film.

Soon afterwards, I saw my first England international match, but it wasn't at Wembley. My 11th birthday present was just the greatest – England v Luxembourg in a World Cup qualifier at Arsenal Stadium, Highbury, on a Thursday night, September 28.

It should have been played on the 27th, but was postponed for a day because of a real pea-souper in London. There was always thick fog in London and often in Hemel, too.

We went on a coach from Rotax, a regular company outing with dads encouraged to take their boys (no girls, obviously). Normally, the trips were over-subscribed and you had to get lucky in a draw, but Dad said it was easy to get tickets this time because the opposition were real crap and we'd already beaten them 9-0 away. By way of proving he wasn't the only one to feel that way, only 33,000 were in the stadium.

I didn't even know where Luxembourg was and it was too small a country to find on the wall map outside the headmaster's office. But it had to be quite a big place to have its own radio station, which Mum sometimes listened to at night because they played lots of new records.

We were sad that Jimmy Greaves wasn't in the team because he'd gone to Italy to play for AC Milan, and the crowd around us standing on the North Bank booed a lot, but Bobby Charlton scored twice in a 4-1 win and immediately became my all-time favourite footballer.

I remember the team, of course: Ron Springett, Jimmy Armfield, Mick McNeil, Peter Swan, Ron Flowers, Bobby Charlton, Ray Pointer, Bryan Douglas, Bobby Robson, Dennis Viollet, Johnny Fantham.

They didn't sell Doodledogs at Arsenal, just tiny tasteless frankfurters fished out of lukewarm water with bits of onion floating in it. But never mind, I had an England rosette the size of a baby's head and a really old and heavy wooden rattle I could just about manage to swing with both hands and make the most horrendous noise.

Dad and Granda used to carry it down to the Bush (Shepherd's, that is) to see the Rangers (Queens Park) before I was born, but I never got to go there.

I never went dog racing, either. They told me how they regularly went to see the greyhounds just after the war. They always backed the Trap 6 dog, who had to wear a black and white striped jacket. But it wasn't for little boys, they said. Or women. Just gambling and drinking with regular crowds of 50,000-plus at Wembley and up to 100,000 at White City Stadium (built for the 1908 Olympics, demolished in 1985), just two miles from Harlesden.

I had to stick to football. No problem there.

Back home, I abandoned Chaulden United and their pitch Down The Field and went a mile or so further afield to get excited watching Hemel Hempstead Town playing in the Delphian League against the likes of Ware, Woodford, Bishop's Stortford and Brentwood.

They weren't much cop said Dad, who of course never set foot in the ground, but it was easy for me and fellow football nut Phil to get in free over the fence near the back entrance to the Crabtree Lane ground and we saw some great games.

We saw a great player, too, in that brilliant little theatre of football (demolished in 1972) near the Plough roundabout, one of my first sporting heroes – Dai Price, a bulky bull-like centre-forward who ran and ran as if on skates and had a forehead made of rock.

To round it off, we took enough pennies with us for a cup of Bovril and the kindly lady who ran the tea bar in the main stand always gave us a free bun each, a round one with lots of currants.

In exchange, we had to promise her to go straight home to our mums after the match or they'd be worried sick.

"Football is the greatest game ever. We invented it, taught the whole world how to play." That's what Granda said.

Granda knew everything in the whole world, but probably not that he would die the week before England won the World Cup in 1966.

20
School Trips

The best thing about a school day trip was the journey. I just loved looking out of the bus window at all the places I'd never seen before, imagining who lived in them, what they did, what their names were. I tried so hard to concentrate, not least in the hope I wouldn't be sick.

Without fail, it was a bit of a let-down when we got to our destination. A total let-down in fact. They were all terrible.

The Tower of London, for starters. How boring was that? It took us ages to get there just to see loads of old buildings, most of which you weren't allowed in. In fact, they didn't even look really old because they'd all been cleaned up.

Must have been the cleanest buildings in London, which at the time was so grubby every time you blew your nose you saw black bits in the snot when you examined your hanky.

We couldn't run around, we had to stick to pathways that were crammed with people, lots of them from foreign countries, dressed in odd clothes, shuffling along in a daze staring at things and pretending to be interested. We just knew they weren't.

There were a few guards dotted around, but no proper soldiers with guns and stuff. Just these geezers called Beefeaters, really old blokes like Granda, dressed in silly bright costumes which just made us laugh.

In fact, they weren't actually Beefeaters, that was just a nickname someone had given them. Something to do with them getting large beef rations in the distant past. No, they were really Yeoman Warders. What was the point of having two names and confusing everyone like us and all those foreigners?

Even more to the point, they were responsible for all the prisoners in the Tower. Except there weren't any. Hadn't been since Hitler's deputy, Rudolf Hess, had dropped in in 1941 and there were no plans to have any in the future, no matter what the crime. No matter if it was someone even scarier than Hess, like The Woman Downstairs, I allowed myself to think.

To be fair, the Beefies seemed quite nice people and tried to tell us what they were all about and told stories of the place, but we couldn't hear them because there were so many of us.

We'd done a bit of studying about the Tower back at school, but everyone had forgotten.

You weren't allowed to sit on the grass so we just stood about eating our packed lunches, chucking bread crusts towards big fat pigeons. I had a sausage roll from the baker's. Treat. They weren't getting any of that.

Then we had to queue for ages and ages in a special bit to see the Crown Jewels, which were just sparkly things you could see in Hemel shop windows except they were a lot older and included real crowns. They had no prices on them so you didn't know if they were valuable or not. I suppose they must be because of all the fuss.

You could buy a book that told you all about it, but it cost too much money. So no one did.

The Science Museum in Kensington was a bit better, but not much. It was nothing but a great big warehouse, really, with old things stuck in it. Most of them of no interest to small children, so you wondered why we were there in the first place.

Perhaps scientists really liked it, but it was hard to tell if there were any of them there on day trips from laboratories. What do scientists look like?

It had lots of very small models of famous locomotives (but no real ones) and even smaller models of cars from years ago in big glass cases like fish tanks, in the front of which were handles you could turn so they went very slowly up and down piddly little bits of track. Dull, or what?

All the exhibits had cards alongside with lots of information so you could read all about them and actually learn something. No one did. Excitement level nil.

In the middle was the big exhibit – the working coal mine, with 'real' working coal trucks, a lift shaft and coal face. Oh, right. Of course it wasn't a bloody coal mine, not in the middle of London. We weren't that stupid.

They were all in Wales, another country and miles away. All the men in Wales were miners and wore torches on their helmets. They had very hard lives, but were always drinking beer and singing. We'd done a project on them. And Egyptians.

Worse still was Bekonscot Model Village, which at least was only about an hour away in Beaconsfield, so there wasn't really time to be sick all over the bus even though Catherine managed it on the way back. All those aniseed balls.

The oldest model village in the world they told us, full of predictable village bits and pieces like thatched houses, churches, post offices, farms and people playing cricket near a pub. All shrunk to the size of a small dolls' house.

Yeah, yeah. Why couldn't we just go to a proper nice village? We were in the Chilterns, there were loads of them. Have a picnic, play ball games like clenched-fist rounders. The girls could look round the church and go in the shop.

The only interesting thing was the model train, which ran right through the place. It was just the job. All the boys wanted to stay at the best points to watch it, like on the little bridges or by the stations, but we had to form a long crocodile so we got to see everything else by winding along the rope-lined paths. Pathetic. There were no other people in the place.

I didn't get to see it all anyway, because I tried to derail a train by putting a windmill across the track. It just seemed a funny idea, but I suppose it wasn't really.

Our teacher, Mr Perfect, saw me, shouted a lot then sent me back to the car park to sit on the coach with the driver, who moaned and moaned about the trip taking so long as he ate his slice of gala pork pie and sipped his tea from a thermos flask, a hanky tucked in the neck of his waistcoat to absorb the inevitable spillage.

Even nearer for a cheap day trip was the hugely depressing building 10 miles away from Hemel down a side street in Tring which housed Tring Museum, a sort of overflow from the Natural History Museum in London, which clearly had no room, nor appetite, for a vast collection of stuffed animals secured by the filthy rich Rothschild family and donated to the nation. Or at least the Tring part of it.

Twice, in successive years, we had to plod around the dark, dismal and draughty interior pretending to be interested in a couple of thousand dead things, lots of them moths in drawers. No handles to turn, let alone a train set. There was surely nowhere in the world more guaranteed to put a child off museums for life.

Let's get back on the bus, sharpish.

Verulamium? Don't get me started. That's what the old Romans called St Albans, nine miles from Hemel, and in its time (up to around 500AD) the third biggest city in the country after London and Cirencester.

That's about all I remember apart from the old ruins we had to look at which were about as spectacular as looking at building site foundations – and we'd all seen enough of those in Chaulden to last several lifetimes, thanks very much.

The walls were no more interesting than any other remnants of more recent walls and the centrepiece, the theatre, was pathetic. Looked like a pond with no water in it. There was a shop there, too, which called itself a museum where they sold bits of broken Roman pottery. What's the point of that? None of us bought any.

Could you imagine getting home and saying: "Here you are, Mum, a small bit broken off the lip of a very old vase. Cost me 3d. Where shall we put it, over there with the cactus?"

Another regular trip to St Albans was much more like it. The Herts County Show was split into two distinct sections – farm machinery and farm animals. They may as well have put up pink and blue signs.

While the girls were off looking at lambs and rabbits, we were climbing over tractors and steam engines and collecting ridiculous amounts of leaflets which were clearly of no lasting interest at all, merely to satisfy our competitive instincts when we compared our bounty back on the bus.

Not one of us would ever get to ride a combine harvester and none of the girls, for that matter, would ever get their hands on another lamb unless it was a small, dead part of it destined to be served with mint sauce and gravy.

But there were lots of places there selling food and drink and some gave us free samples, bits of lovely smelly cheese which I'd never tasted before and cold pork sausages on pointy sticks, which saved the day.

With one notable exception, we never went anywhere for longer than a day. But what an exception that was.

St Mary's Bay was a different game entirely, not just for me, but all 30-odd of us who headed off to the Kent coast and St Mary's Holiday Camp (renamed the School Journey Centre in 1965, demolished five years later).

It was apparently ideal for exploring the delights of Canterbury and Folkestone, Romney Marsh and Rye. Places we'd never heard of. One of them had a cathedral, but then so did St Albans and that was just up the road. So no big deal.

For many of us it was the first time away from home without our parents, or at least a close relative.

We went for five days during the Easter holidays. Mum packed me a small leather suitcase with appropriate clothing, plus a couple of packets of ginger nuts and some sweets. She gave me a small purse with some money in it, but I can't remember how much – only that all the kids had to take the same amount because that was fair.

We sort of knew where we were off to by the time we went because teacher Mr Smith had pinned a big map of Kent on the wall of the classroom and put big rings round the places we were to visit. They were all about 100 miles from Hemel.

We had to attend an after-school Pre School Trip Briefing to tell us even more. Parents were invited, but mine didn't fancy going. You'll be all right, they said.

Predictably, we sang all the way.

"The wheels on the bus go round and round,
Round and round,
Round and round.
The wheels on the bus go round and round,
All day long.

"The horn on the bus goes beep, beep, beep,
Beep, beep, beep,
Beep, beep, beep.
The horn on the bus goes beep, beep, beep,
All day long."

Etc., etc., etc.

It didn't seem to bother anyone that we were actually on a train from Victoria and weren't due to be bus-bound until arriving at Dover station. By which time we all felt sick and Catherine had predictably chucked up again. More aniseed balls.

I suppose no one knew any train songs? Oh yes, they did. As soon as we got on the coach:

"The runaway train came down the track and she blew she blew,
The runaway train came down the track and she blew she blew,
The runaway train came down the track
Her whistle wide and her throttle back
And she blew, blew, blew, blew, blew."

The singing long exhausted and the coach coming to a halt, no one was prepared for the sight of one of the country's first holiday camps when we eventually got there after what seemed hours and hours. And most certainly was.

It looked like a prison in a field, the other side of the Dymchurch Road from the stony beach. It was absolutely huge and truly forbidding.

Based on military camp designs, it could accommodate around 1,000 children in about a dozen concrete dormitories, with names like Windsor, Ascot, Birkenhead and Leeds. The place was packed all summer long with school parties from all over the country.

Girls one end, boys the other, with their own communal washrooms and toilets. Each of us freezing cold on our camp beds.

The food was the worst in the whole world, served on long trestle tables covered in bird shit from the creatures roosting in the wooden beams of the ceiling. It was always stone cold, brought in on trolleys from a different building that wasn't even close. I can't remember anything we ate, except the porridge. No one could ever forget that.

All of us spent all our pocket money on biscuits from the camp shop because we were hungry all the time. But I did send a postcard home with the place looking really sunny.

Having a nice time, I said, in case Mum was worried. None of us would ever worry our mums. I could always tell her what it was really like when I got back.

We had plenty of room, though, and when we weren't on trips we could do much as we liked on the massive playing fields. We had one organised football match and played a team from south London, who were unbelievable. Whacked us about 6-0, bringing comparisons, but probably only from me who'd read all about it, of the Hungarians beating England 6-3 at Wembley back in 1953.

The best bit was going to Dover Castle, which was really interesting. A real castle with real battlements from which we were told we could see France. We might have done but for the fog. It was all we could do to see the coach park.

We even got to walk along the windy cliffs. But we weren't allowed anywhere near the edge, which would have been so much more exciting.

We went to Canterbury Cathedral too (big and boring except the downstairs creepy part), and Dungeness Lighthouse (not allowed to climb the stairs) and some old village church which was even colder than being back at the camp.

We were given these really heavy black crayons and thickish sheets of paper and encouraged to take brass rubbings from plaques in the floor, which were to be displayed on the classroom wall the minute we got back. I lost mine, but it wasn't destined for a place in the limelight anyway.

I would have liked to have gone swimming in the sea one day, but we weren't allowed because it was too cold. We were getting used to feeling that way, we reckoned. We walked along the beach and saw a few ships in the distance, but that was about it. No fairs or amusement arcades. The whole place was grim and dead. The last place you'd want to go on holiday, I told Mum and Dad.

All the kids from all over the camp got together on the last night for a big campfire and sing-song, which everyone loved if only because we were all warm. The soup wasn't, though.

The people in charge of the camp gave out awards for best campers, but I didn't win anything. None of us from Chaulden did, but they were only bags of sweets anyway. I just wanted to go home. We all did.

"Never went on a school trip in my life. Too busy learning how to read and write." That's what Granda said.

Granda knew everything in the whole world, although that's stretching it when it comes to school trips.

21

Having A Lovely Time

Much of my last year at junior school was focused on being in love with my first girlfriend, Ruth. I can only suppose other boys were similarly attracted to classmates, but of course we never mentioned it.

No boy would ever admit he'd gone soppy on a girl. They were virtually aliens. Boys wouldn't talk about such things, not with each other and certainly not with parents.

It wasn't right. They would never understand. It was just silly, after all, wasn't it?

She was so lovely. I always wanted to kiss her, but of course I never did, never really knew how to go about it. I mean, where do you start with a girl when you're both 11 years old?

Do you ask her for a kiss, or just sort of lean forward towards her? And then what? You've only ever kissed old powdery relatives before, that's the absolute extent of your displays of affection.

What do you say, what do you do with your arms, or her arms? Do you just grab them and hope for the best?

I held her hand once when we crossed a road, but she let go as soon as we reached the other side and that was my lot. All I know is I wished it had been a very much wider road.

A few times we went to the Saturday Morning Pictures together at the brand-new Odeon Cinema in Marlowes (opened in 1960, a Wetherspoon's pub since 1998), where for 6d each (now 48p) we'd sample the delights of Zorro and Flash Gordon, Felix the Cat, Hopalong Cassidy and an ever-changing list of other firm favourites.

I liked The Three Stooges best, but in truth it didn't much matter what was on the screen. It was a giant kids' party, unrivalled bargain-priced excitement at a time when parents in places like Hemel had little spare cash to dish out for kiddies' entertainment. No one was ill-treated or half-starved, but food had to come before frivolity.

If it was your birthday, you had to stand up and the whole packed-out cinema would sing Happy Birthday To You and you went bright red, but got a free Eldorado ice-cream. Never happened to me.

Ruth and I always put our money together and bought a bag of Butterkist popcorn and some Kia-Ora orange squash and sometimes a bar of Cadbury's Fruit & Nut. All from a small counter in the ticket hall where on the wall was a big photo of a few builders, two men in suits and an actress from Hollywood, Lauren Bacall, who'd laid the Odeon's foundation stone in 1959.

I'd get on the town centre-bound Bream bus at the bottom of Long Chaulden and Ruth's dad would be waiting with her at the bus stop at the end of their road, Roseheath, five minutes away. He'd be there again to take her home when we came back from town, and I carried on to my stop.

Mum and Dad loved me going and went on and on about all the great times they'd had at the pictures – sometimes called the flicks, maybe the flea pit, never the cinema. And always films, never movies.

They had firm favourites like It's A Wonderful Life, All About Eve, Road To Rio, The Postman Always Rings Twice, The Best Years Of Our Lives and Mum's all-time favourite, Gone With The Wind. Clark Gable and Vivien Leigh. Films don't get better than that, she said, what seemed like hundreds of times.

If they enjoyed it so much, I wondered why they didn't ever go to the pictures anymore. Seemed they only went when they were courting and I wasn't really sure what that was about except it probably meant kissing.

Mind you, they also apparently loved dancing and they didn't do that either, unless it was a wedding reception or something and they'd had a few. In Dad's case, it had to be quite a few. Mum said he had two left feet, neither of which functioned at all well on a dance floor.

They didn't seem to go out anywhere together, just the two of them, because I suppose they didn't have much money to spare and anyway they were lumbered with looking after Sally and me, although they never said it like that. Babysitting was a foreign word. No one, but no one, ever paid someone else to look after their own children. That's how it was.

They did have a trip to Watford once to get some Christmas presents for us, so we couldn't go and instead went to Aunty Laura's. I was excited for them only because it entailed a ride on the 301 bus for seven miles along the A41.

The 708 and 719 Green Line services also went that way, but they were dearer because they didn't stop at all the bus stops and were for people in a hurry. Dad said they were never in so much of a hurry that he'd pay more money for going down the same road to the same place on the same day.

We were happy they had a very good time and even had a pink salmon sandwich and a nice cup of tea at a little cafe near the Bakerloo Line station in the High Street.

The days of cowboys and Indians were over. Consigned to the annals of my personal history, along with the Dinky cars and marbles, polio jabs and dustmen-worshipping. And pissing in inappropriate places, come to think of it.

Now we branched out, spending more and more time in the fields and woods rather than the streets and alleys. Jocketts Woods, five minutes along Chaulden Terrace, the road opposite our house, became the more regular centre of our miniature universe.

There, we climbed trees like the hundreds of grey squirrels who rightly called the area home, and carved our initials in the bark of the trunks. Sometimes we wrote words like 'Shit' and 'Arse' instead and promised each other no one would say who'd done it should an adult take us to task.

We broke down bushes and ripped out foliage much loved by resident hedgehogs to make lean-to camps. We pretended we were African explorers and needed to hide from rampaging lions and people with bones through their noses armed with spears who would inevitably stand us in huge pots and make soup out of us, like we saw in The Hotspur.

The bendy beech branches all around were perfect for making our own bows and arrows, wrapping small bits of lead wire around the ends so the arrows would go further and more accurately in the hope of claiming a 'kill'.

The target was invariably an innocent passer-by using the pathway along the edge of the woods. Preferably an elderly woman carrying heavy shopping bags up the steep hill who wouldn't be able to chase after us.

We turned that same pathway into a winter sports centre whenever it snowed, hurtling down the icy slope on metal trays with no hope of steering them in any particular direction, crashing into others at the bottom, a giggling pile of wet winter woolies.

In spring, we stole birds' eggs from their nests and took them home to rest in shoeboxes lined with cotton wool until they began to stink and our mothers chucked them in the bin.

But most fun of all was building fires. The scrubland around the woods was ideal. Dry and light, it was easy to get a small blaze going with the simple aid of a magnifying glass, and we all had one of those. Should things get out of hand, there were always plenty of us to stamp out the flames.

Mostly, that is. On two occasions during one summer holiday, the fire took charge and frightened the life out of us. Each time, a 999 call from the phone box by the path ensured the fire brigade turned up and took over while we watched, hearts beating, totally enthralled, from our treetop hideaways and later denied all knowledge of any involvement.

Most of the time, anything untoward like that was blamed on the Big Kids rather than us. They sat on the swings near the entrance to the woods, smoking and swearing and just looking scary. Some of them had leather jackets and they all wore tight-fitting trousers and had hair swept back with lots of Brylcreem.

Mum and Dad said we shouldn't have anything to do with them because they were Teddy Boys and could be naughty. There had been lots about them in the papers, causing trouble at dances and the seaside. All of them carried knives.

But they were more insistent that we kept well clear of any 'funny men', who apparently were attracted to a combination of woods and small children, although we were never told exactly why or what we were supposed to be looking for. Or, indeed, if they ever came looking for us.

Some of the Big Kids were all right, though, and we met them when we went to the youth club at Chaulden House. They drank coffee and smoked a lot while they taught us how to play snooker, despite the obvious handicap of half the balls being missing along with the tips of the cues and the rack for the remaining reds.

They also put records on the gramophone, the first time I'd ever seen one apart from at a family do in a church hall. We were all fascinated, but not allowed to touch it because they knew we were too young. We'd lied about our ages and shouldn't really have been in there until we were 12.

By way of complete contrast, almost the furthest point from Jocketts Woods (more accurately also known as Shrub Hill Common) in Chaulden were the watercress beds of the Gadespring company, which lay below the main railway line and alongside the Bulbourne.

They stretched for four acres, at one time producing a fifth of the entire nation's supply. Production stopped in 1991.

The cress was regularly cut in spring and summer by men in waist-high waders wielding large scissors and was then boxed in twine-secured bunches by their wives sitting in a small wooden hut, then sent by train to Euston and subsequently Covent Garden Market.

Dad said it was for posh people to put in their sandwiches or tear up and put it over salads, a bit like grass cuttings. He said it tasted horrible, so we never had any. Never even pinched it.

What we did have in that idyllic part of Hemel were our usual unexciting sandwiches and maybe a flask of Robinson's Lemon Barley Water. Sustenance for spending many an hour there, chosen because it was the easiest place for hauling ourselves up the steep railway embankment in defiance of any number of deathly warning signs.

Picturesque it may have been, but all we really cared about was the next 4-6-2 wheel-arrangement locomotive enveloping us in smoke as it carted its carriages along the London, Midland and Scottish region of the nationalised British Railway tracks on its way to the Euston terminus.

Or else in the opposite direction to Wolverton, Birmingham and maybe beyond to the huge engineering works at Crewe and its six-way junction, and other mystical places in the North.

None of us had ever been to the North, or met anyone from the North. Or even met anyone who had met anyone from the North. Where the hell was it? Where did it start and finish? What was the point?

Jam sandwiches and a Penguin biscuit aside, we all had a notepad and an Ian Allan ABC train-spotting book. Almost every boy had an Ian Allan, which listed all the names and numbers of the region's engines.

As you spotted each train in busy periods, you'd scrawl down its number in the notepad, then use your six-inch ruler to underline your capture in the ABC list when there was a lull in the action, a neater and permanent undisputed record of absolutely no use at all.

Another vantage point was further along the line, at the other side of the station towards Apsley and ultimately Euston. Here, we sat on the bank near the bridge and Roughdown Common, part of which was once a chalk mine, and sometimes got really close by scurrying down the bank and recklessly across the tracks towards the Boxmoor gasometers.

Huge and threatening, they towered over the start of the branch line which had once weaved its way for eight miles north-east towards Harpenden. With the locomotives (called Puffing Annies) leading the way, it called at Heath Park Halt, then puffed along behind West Herts Hospital to Midland Railway Station, and on to Cupid Green and Redbourn.

Known as the Nicky Line, and with nine stations in all, the service ended in 1947, although it continued to serve the gasometers until 1959. A shame I never got a Puffing Annie in my Ian Allan book.

Inevitably, non-spotters simply laughed out loud at this outrageous way of squandering days of precious childhood. And had every right to do so. But what completely uncomplicated escapism it was at the time.

Much less fun than train-spotting books, though only marginally less popular, were the range of I-Spy publications, the attraction of which was completely lost on me.

Available in good bookshops everywhere, and presumably inferior bookshops too, they were also 'spotting' publications supposedly written by a Red Indian called Big Chief I-Spy, in reality Charles Warrell, a Mansfield headmaster, later followed by an antiques dealer from Islington.

The series (worldwide sales 25 million!) included such gems as I-Spy Cars, I-Spy Churches, I-Spy Dogs and about 30 other small books, ownership of which made you a member of the I-Spy Tribe.

The idea was to spot a selection of listed and pictured items for which points were gained according to scarcity. You got a lot more for spotting a Japanese Shiba Inu than a corgi, for instance, or a church on some obscure Scottish island rather than Westminster Abbey.

Completed books could be sent off to the publishers at Wigwam-by-the-Water, London EC4, in the hope of being awarded a badge and a feather.

A couple of boys in our class were fans, but they got laughed at even more than the train-spotters.

"Train-spotting. Why would anyone do that?" That's what Granda said.
Granda knew everything in the whole world, although he was happy to remain ignorant in this respect.

22

Plenty To Report

Schoolwork was still no great problem for me and the results in the final year were much the same as previous years.

There were 111 children in the year group by now, split into three classes, each of them housed in temporary buildings because the school population had already boomed way beyond what the planning 'experts' had predicted just a few years earlier.

The school, not yet 10 years old, was already out of date. It wasn't just full to bursting, it had actually burst.

Thanks to the same people who hadn't allowed for a four-wheel boom and the consequential steady disappearance of front gardens and a parallel increase in sales of concrete, presumably.

Amid the mainly As and Bs for attainment and effort, I got the usual unflattering teachers' comments thrown in: "He tends to take things much too easily"... "He spoils good work by unnecessary haste"...

Blimey, I was fourth in English and third in arithmetic, the only two subjects deemed worthy of consideration for the final year-group placings, which meant third place overall.

Third out of 111. Must do better. Do me a favour.

English was becoming more interesting by the day. I actually enjoyed lessons on basic sentence construction, learning about subjects and objects, verbs and nouns and various clauses.

We were allowed to make up our own sentences – the sillier the better! – and teacher would chalk the words up on the blackboard, then show which part of the sentence they each formed.

Collective nouns were even more fun. We could all guess at herds of cows, packs of Brownies and even a shoal of roach. But hands up all those who knew of a mischief of mice, an ambush of widows or a rhumba of rattlesnakes?

Reading matter changed, too. Out with Enid Blyton and Biggles, in with Tolkien's The Hobbit and Stevenson's Treasure Island, Kipling's Just So Stories and Crompton's Just William series, featuring schoolboy William Brown, perhaps the poshest toe rag ever.

Even poetry was quite rightly on the learning list. What kid didn't just love TS Eliot's Old Possum's Book of Practical Cats or The Nonsense

Verse of Edward Lear?

> "The Owl and the Pussy-cat went to sea
> In a beautiful pea green boat.
> They took some honey, and plenty of money,
> Wrapped up in a five pound note.
> The Owl looked up to the stars above,
> And sang to a small guitar,
> 'O lovely Pussy! O Pussy my love,
> What a beautiful Pussy you are, you are,
> What a beautiful Pussy you are!'"

As well as reading and writing, I was beginning to enjoy arithmetic a lot more. We'd long since moved on from simple adding, subtracting and multiplying. Long division was much more taxing, then we learnt all about fractions and decimals.

Weights and measures, based on pounds and ounces and extending to stones, hundredweights and tons, was fascinating. So, too, the liquid equivalent of fluid ounces, gills, pints, quarts, gallons, pecks and bushels, plus lengths from inches, feet, yards, rods, chains, furlongs and on to miles and leagues.

The mathematical complexities of having a currency of pounds, shillings and pence based on 240 pence equalling a pound soon became painfully apparent to all of us.

And, topping the lot, the challenge of mastering Roman numerals, which even then (MCMLXII) seemed the most sensible system of all, even if its modern usage seemed to be restricted to film credits, clock faces, the identification of kings and queens and the introduction pages of books (not this one).

To test myself, I got a strip of unwanted wallpaper out of the shed and wrote out the entire final Football League Division 1 table for the 1961-62 season, won by Ipswich Town, in Roman numerals and showed it to Dad. He said Ipswich would never win it again in his lifetime (they didn't) and had no idea what the numerals were all about.

I even explained how lucky the table was for me, since there wasn't a 0 in sight, and the Romans had no character to represent zero. He was none the wiser, but I said I'd take it to school and show the teacher, Mr Smith.

Dad said teacher would only think I was a flashy little git. And an expressionless Mr Smith seemed to confirm that as he tucked my

157

painstaking work under the paperweight on his desk by his cold bacon sandwiches wrapped, as ever, in re-used greaseproof paper.

Top grades aside, I got my usual C in music and another one for scripture (I didn't even know we got marked for that), but a surprise B in art and crafts, where I was still totally devoid of talent despite a bold but inevitably unrealistic effort at making a Panzer tank out of a Coco Pops box and a straw.

All the other kids regularly had their paintings pinned on the classroom wall, but I managed it only the once.

We were given the task of painting a cat in an overgrown garden, an exercise way, way beyond anything I could manage. So in desperation I just splattered the whole piece of paper with green paint. Chucked it on. Then, in black, I painted two blobs in the middle as eyes. Took me about 10 minutes, then I stared out of the window for half an hour.

Mr Smith loved it to death. Couldn't get the drawing pins out of his drawer fast enough, went on and on about boldness, ambition, spontaneity, originality, my hidden ability.

Not as hidden as the cat, mate.

It was a farce. Any potential love affair with art started and finished at that very moment, especially as some of the kids were really talented. John was a genius, particularly painting birds, but he always wore a red Man Utd shirt underneath his regulation white one so everyone thought he was a nutter. Manchester? They didn't even play in London, did they? Come on.

Malcolm was almost as gifted artistically, with rockets and spaceships his speciality to the extent of my football obsession. He'd paint every tiny detail then happily tell everyone all about it. The role of every bit of visible metal, it seemed, before he started on fuel and orbits and conditions beyond Earth.

All us boys were into astronauts and stuff since Yuri Gagarin became the first man to travel into outer space, in April 1961.

Malcolm would explain to us (and an enraptured teacher, as it happens) about the Russian Sputnik exploration programme, then go on and on about planets and solar systems and meteors and stars, even telling us man would land on the Moon in the next 10 years. Malcolm also reckoned it would be an American, not a Russian like everyone else was saying.

I told Dad all about Malcolm, hoping he'd be suitably impressed. Dad said keep away from him.

I didn't, though. In fact we joined Chaulden Chess Club together and that was brilliant. My Real Uncle Roy taught me how to play when they came over one Sunday afternoon and he bought me a travelling set in a small wooden box. I was hooked.

It was only a few pence to join the club, which met one evening a week in Chaulden Hall. They supplied the boards and the huge wooden pieces and you were allowed to ask for help if you needed it because everyone else was so much better. And mostly quite old. Very old.

You'd play a different person every time and if the game wasn't finished when the session ended, you just made a note of where all the pieces were on special sheets of paper with boards drawn on, then continue the following week.

I would have gone more often, but none of my other mates knew how to play or had any interest in learning, even though the adults at the club would have taught them for free. My lovely travelling set never actually travelled anywhere at all, not for years.

Malcolm was a good swimmer, too, and a regular at Churchill's Swimming Baths, where we all learnt to swim. In our last year, we'd go by coach one morning a week for school lessons paid for by the council, who must have thought we'd otherwise all end up face down in the Grand Union, which would have caused a right row.

The water in the open-air pool in Park Road (now the Sportspace complex) was often freezing and there was no hot water or heating in the changing rooms. But we all loved it and the baths themselves became something of a kids' social meeting place at weekends, everyone – girls as well as boys, almost uniquely at our age – gathering on the large grass surrounds, sitting sipping hot Bovril in their woollen swimming gear from Woolies, whether taking the plunge or not.

Mum encouraged me to go as often as possible, but never resisted giving me the same dire warnings as I tucked my towel and trunks under my arm. Never use anyone else's towel or you'll get a terrible disease. Make sure you dry between your feet or you'll get athlete's foot and be unable to walk. Dry everywhere else, too, or you'll get terrible rheumatism like that woman in the Co-op.

I survived to get my 25 yards certificate, joined Hemel Hempstead Swimming & Diving Club and Mum sewed a big cloth badge on my trunks, which weighed almost as much as the trunks. Next up 50 yards, 100 yards and onwards to the cherished mile, which got us achievers a mention at school assembly, a slot normally reserved for those who'd shamefully transgressed in a toilet-related way. A lifelong love of water was born.

The only drawback going to Churchill's was the huge number of bikes regularly stolen from outside, even if they had a lock and chain. The Gazette was always running stories, but no one did anything about it. You could hardly have a copper standing there all day.

Not that it bothered me. I didn't have one.

We'd sometimes go to pubs on the way to Churchill's because they weren't open on the way back. Yes, another waste of time favoured by small boys: collecting beer mats. I reckon more than half of us were temporarily tegestologists (Mr Smith told us what it meant), for no apparent reason.

It's not as though they may be valuable, like stamps or coins. Or even that you'd spotted the Royal Scot steaming along the railway tracks on its seven-hour journey to Glasgow, or a Japanese Shiba Inu, doing whatever one of those did.

I kept the mats in a box in my room. I had hundreds of them until I just got fed up one day and gave them all to Trevor up the road, whose mum promptly put them in the dustbin along with his own not-very-prized collection.

We gently tapped on the public bar windows of Boxmoor pubs like The Grapes in Green End Road, then on to the Post Office Arms (always known as The Patch) in Puller Road, the Three Blackbirds and the Steam Coach in St John's Road and the Anchor along Beechfield Road (closed in 2010).

Without fail, a kindly customer would come out and hand us a couple of mats filched from the bar, different shapes and sizes, different breweries – Flowers, Bass, Whitbread, Ind Coope, Fremlins, Truman's, McMullen's, Benskins, Friary Meux, Charrington's.

In the towel they went, along with the swimming trunks, any duplicates destined for possible swapping in the school playground, along with the cigarette cards, Golliwog badges, comics and stamps.

We also trawled the pubs for a different reason. Round the back, some of them would leave empties waiting to go back to the brewery which we would pinch, then take them to the off-sales attached to a different pub (but same brewery) to get back the bottle deposit money. If there was any beer in the bottom, we would of course drink it. Anyone would do the same. That's how it was.

The only other time beer touched my sensitive young lips was when I had a sip of Granda's bottle of Guinness after I'd won the 100 yards race at the Rotax family open day, a marvellous annual occasion on the factory's playing fields, with a funfair, stalls and loads of free food and drink.

But my biggest sprinting triumph came during my final junior school sports day, beating David, who everyone had expected to be first to the bit of string held across the end of the track. But he wasn't, though not by much.

It meant I qualified to represent the school in the local district sports event, held at Broadfield School, across town near the Queen's Square shopping centre in Adeyfield, the new town's oldest centre and the site visited by HRH in 1952 to lay the foundation stone.

I wanted Mum and Dad to come because they never went to a sports day and hadn't been to see me beat David and I really thought I was going to win again and be a proper champion, but they didn't make that, either. Too busy.

Just as well, I suppose. I was last. All the other kids from my school were sympathetic, saying things like I wasn't at my best and my bit of the track was muddiest. Nice, but it didn't help. I was still last.

"You won the holiday camp race, you won the Rotax race, you won the school race. Everyone gets beat sometime." That's what Granda said.

Granda knew everything in the whole world, although running races were never his strongpoint.

23

Presents By Post

Granda was never far away, even if it was 22 miles and we so rarely saw them. Every Saturday morning I waited eagerly for the postman to turn up and deposit mainly uninteresting dispatches onto the doormat. But within them was always one envelope addressed to Master Stephen F Riches. My magical present.

Usually, it was a couple of packets of stamps. One of the best presents I ever got was a stamp album during a Harlesden visit round about birthday time and Granda seemed determined to fill it up for me in the coming years. Every boy had a stamp album.

The pages within the leather cover were fascinating, each topped with the name of the country, its capital city, population, currency and size (in square miles). At the back were maps showing where everywhere was and I studied them intently, comparing the size and shapes of the countries on my globe, another Granda gift, this time from a junk shop in Kensal Green, where he'd got the Chinese vase.

I carefully attached hinges to the latest stamps (never lick and stick, they become valueless) and stuck them on their designated pages within the album in neat rows, pretending I'd actually been to those places and bought them in their post offices, strolling inside wearing a panama hat.

I learned all the capitals of all the countries, from the Republics of Dahomey (capital, Porto-Novo) and Malagasy (Antananarivo) to Spanish Guinea (St Isabel) and Nyasaland (Zomba), and developed an unrealistic ambition to visit the Suvadive Islands (Hithadhoo).

The globe sat on a small table in my bedroom, showing England as the tiniest of countries. You could just about see London written on it, but not Harlesden. And no Hemel Hempstead, let alone Chaulden.

But Granda pointed out Japan and I showed it to Tojo when I took it on one visit, who pretended to be more interested in his bowels. I should have shown him the Amazon, I suppose, but I didn't really know which bit because it was so big.

Sometimes Granda might instead send a three-bob (3s/15p, now £3) postal order so I could save up for bits to add to my train set (he loved trains too). For that money you could buy characters like men with flags or shovels, or maybe a set of buffer stops or a whistle sign and a couple of trackside safety lamps.

But you needed a few more pennies to get a goods shed, a water tank or a passenger bridge and even more for really exciting accessories like a four-way rail junction, a trackside crane or an engine turntable and tunnels of varying lengths, painted green on top as though you'd be fooled into thinking it was grass.

The bigger shops sold everything we wanted and we went into Hemel town centre far more now that we thought we were really grown up, scouring every store to spend our pocket money. Each of us spent every single penny every week. It was like a challenge, as though if we had any left over it would be deducted from the next Saturday morning pay-out.

Strangely, we never ventured into Hemel's lovely little Old Town, the cluster of buildings around the 12th Century St Mary's Church. It was never mentioned, but it was like we didn't belong. That was how it was before the builders moved in to create our new homes and habitat around it. Somewhere to be respected, to be left alone.

Not so the newly revamped and thriving Marlowes, where Taylor & McKenna was a must, with its huge array of toys and games, arts and crafts, so big it was on two floors. We'd spend ages in there, compiling our mental wish-lists before moving on to Peter Spivey, a marvellous sports shop packed with kit and equipment and more football boots than you could imagine. And tennis rackets, for some reason.

But of all the shops, us kids preferred Woolworth's because it was easier to pinch the sweets. The Saturday staff were all schoolgirls who didn't seem to care what you did. It wasn't their shop was it, and they were always standing about chatting to the smoking Big Kids, not looking out for the likes of us.

So we just grabbed anything, but avoided chocolate that would melt in the pocket. A dead giveaway – you wouldn't put chocolate in your pocket if you'd paid for it, would you?

Airfix model aircraft kits were easy to acquire, too. They came in handy plastic bags, just the right size for a coat pocket. Every boy had a collection of them, legally or otherwise. I had Spitfires and Hurricanes, Messerschmitts and Focke-Wulfs, all hanging from drawing pin-supported cotton lines on my bedroom ceiling.

Dad thought they looked great. Mum thought they took a lot of dusting and one day knocked the propeller off my favourite, a Tiger Moth, just after I'd finished putting the transfers on. She seemed upset, so I pretended not to be cross although I was a little bit.

Dad wrote to Granda every week, staying seated at the kitchen table after tea while Mum cleared the table and did the washing-up. And peered out of the window, of course. Just in case she missed anything that really ought to be shouted from the nearest rooftops, or at least whispered in Aunty Laura's always-receptive ears.

From the table drawer he produced his Sheaffer fountain pen filled with blue-black Parker's Quink, never any other make or colour. Black and red ink were for business, green for loonies, he said. He never had a business or knew any loonies, as far as I could tell. So blue-black it was.

And always on white Basildon Bond lined notepaper made down the road at the Apsley Mills factory of John Dickinson & Co, the town's largest employer, which had become a munitions factory during the war, making mainly petrol tanks for long-range bombers and strips of foil to be dropped by planes to confuse enemy radar systems.

But now back to what it did best. Best paper in the world, son, he told me every time before I was sent off on a 200-yard run to put the letter in the pillar box safe and sound once I'd affixed a stamp and licked its matching gummed envelope addressed to Mr and Mrs FC Riches, 11 Springwell Avenue, Harlesden, London NW10.

Dad had brilliant handwriting, the only testimony to the teaching of those terrifying nuns.

"You can tell a man by his handwriting. Sloppy writing, sloppy attitude to life. I can sum up a man by the way he writes his name." That's what Granda said.

Granda knew everything in the whole world, although his own letters could have been written more neatly had he bought himself a new nib for his worn-out fountain pen.

24

Granda And Colin

One week, there was no letter back from Harlesden. Granda had been rushed into hospital. People were always 'rushed' there. No one ever went at a reasonable pace, even if it was only a broken arm or something and they actually went by bus. But this was rushing for real.

It was February 1962, just a week before he was due to retire.

Apparently, Granda had left work early because of stomach pains. He'd never left early in his life, not in the 43 years he'd worked there. Worse, he'd had to keep stopping as he walked back from the sorting office and a woman from the greengrocers by Jubilee Clock had helped him the last few hundred yards home.

He got there mid-morning, climbed the stairs and promptly collapsed to his knees on the kitchen floor. He was in a right two and eight.

Poor Nanny, herself off work with a sprained wrist after tripping over in the High Street, tried not to panic and went next door where she knew they had a phone and the neighbour called an ambulance.

They kept him in Park Royal Hospital. Nanny got the bus back home and the woman next door let her phone Dad's factory, where he was summoned to the manager's office to take the call. Everyone knew it was serious. The men on the shop floor weren't allowed phone calls otherwise. Not even if they'd been made up to charge hands and got paid holidays.

Dad left work and went straight to London.

Mum tried to tell me all this without scaring me when I got home from school. By then, she had arranged for me to go and stay with her sister, Real Aunty Brenda, and Real Uncle Roy at their house on the other side of Hemel, in Leverstock Green, an old established part of town. Tile Kiln Lane. A bit nobby. Not a council house in sight.

She was off to join Dad in Harlesden and Sally would stay with a friend over the road from our house. Mum had packed each of us a suitcase full of clothes, like we were going on holiday.

Anything but. It was a terrible time and all I could think of were terrible things, especially as I sat on my own on the No. 320 bus for 25 minutes each way.

It didn't even seem to matter that Dad wouldn't let me look after the school hamster, Horatio, during the coming half term in case it died on us and we had to buy another one. I'd been very disappointed about that, especially after I'd won the chance to do so in the school raffle. I'd never been in a raffle before.

Now I felt strangely uncomfortable, scared even, walking up the hill past our house with no one in it, so I walked the long way round the block along Jocketts Road to school feeling a bit lost and tearful, which wasn't like me at all.

It was like that for nearly two weeks until Mum and Dad came back and told me Granda would be OK. In all that time, I had no idea what really had happened, just my aunt and uncle saying he'd had an operation, they'd been in touch on the phone every day, all was well.

Turns out, he'd had a blockage in his bum. Doctors had cleared it up. Doctors always know best. No problem. Don't worry. Routine, happens all the time. He's never felt better. And now he was retired he could put his feet up.

He just has to have a little bag with him all the time, his own private toilet tucked inside his trousers. It's easy to empty, think nothing of it. Just don't tell anyone, especially not the other kids. They wouldn't understand and Granda might be embarrassed.

So no one spoke of it.

It was the worst thing that had happened to me by a million miles. Worse than Slowcoach rotting in his shell. Worse than Mum crying about that money. Worse than not kissing Ruth.

I don't think I realised at the time, but I suppose I was growing up. Things mattered which never had before, like suddenly developing a great thirst for knowledge outside of football statistics.

I was more interested in other people and what they thought. If I didn't know something, it would irritate me until I found out. And, for the first time, I actually noticed what I was wearing, like my lovely new purple jeans. The first long trousers I ever had. How I wished I was allowed to wear them to school.

They came out of a catalogue, I don't know which. All the mums had at least a Kays catalogue and probably Grattan, Littlewoods and Freemans as well. Everything came on the never-never, just like those expensive electrical things in the kitchen.

I put the jeans on when Granda and Nanny came to stay with us on his return from hospital with his colostomy bag. He certainly didn't mind talking about it, quite the reverse. It was always called Colin and always supposed to elicit much laughter.

Colin needs to go for a walk. Colin's been drinking too much. Colin hums a bit – though that may have been more as a result of the raw onion Granda always carried around in the pocket of his grey (always grey) cardigan.

He would take a bite now and again then re-wrap it in his handkerchief, one of those he got one Christmas with F sewn into the corner. You just knew Mum wasn't in favour.

Granda's adoption of Colin almost precisely coincided with me leaving Chaulden Junior School, just a few weeks after sitting the 11-Plus exam.

Lots of people made a big fuss about it, but my parents hardly mentioned it and I don't remember it being much different to the tests we regularly had in the classroom, like every week.

It was a complete irrelevance. We all knew the kids in the top class would all go to the grammar schools, but we were assured all the other schools were just as good and anyway there were so many other things going on in the minds of an 11-year-old.

"Don't grow up too fast. You've got millions of things to learn, so take your time and take them all in." That's what Granda said.

Granda knew everything in the whole world, although he probably didn't have time to tell me all he knew.

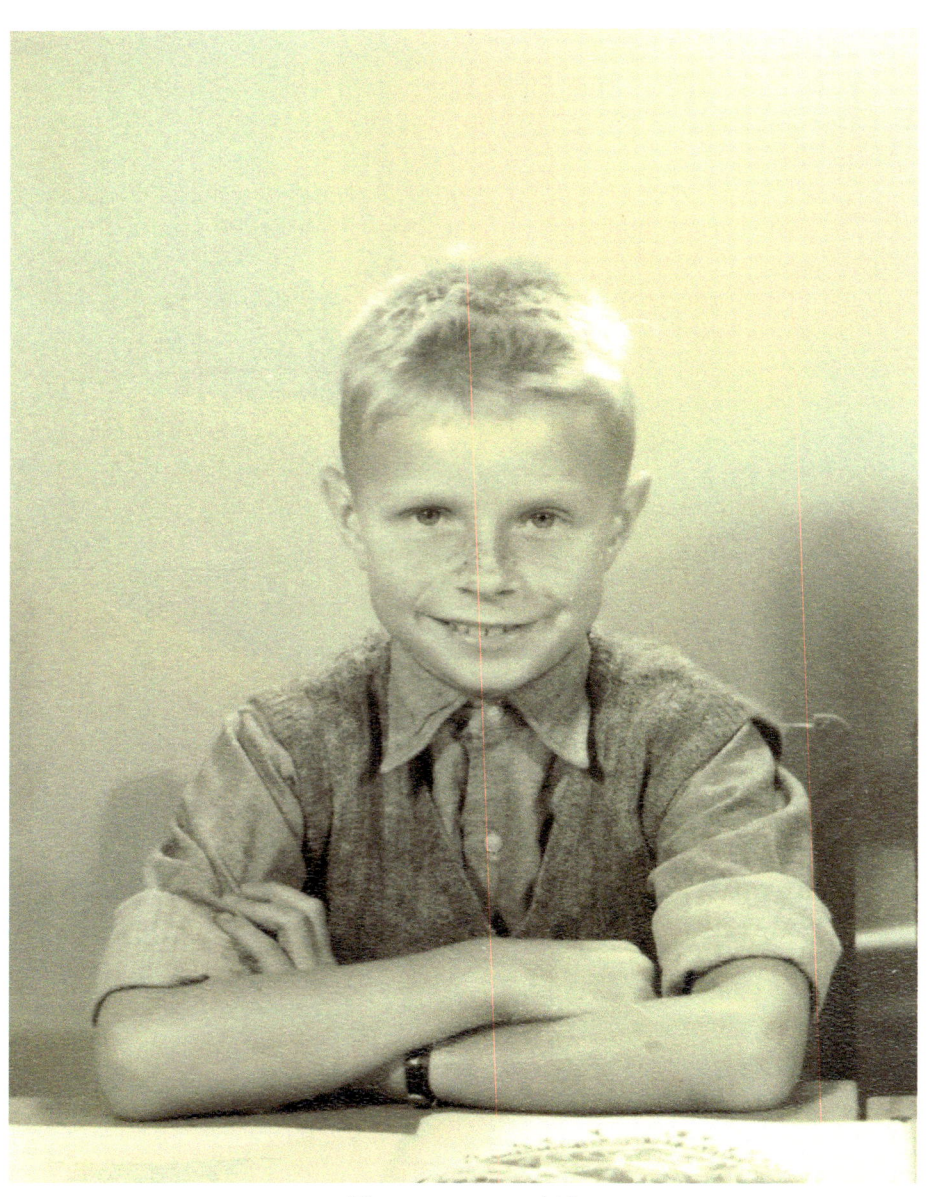

All grown up, aged 11.

25
...And The Ending

I remember the last day at Chaulden Juniors so well. The 9am start, as usual. Friday, July 20, 1962. Mum walked me up the road, something she hadn't done for years. To make sure I was all right. It was a big day, after all. Don't forget to thank your teacher. Give her a kiss.

As if from outer space, the Headmaster, Mr Chapman, appeared in front of us like a superior human being, seemingly suddenly distrustful of his minion alongside. No way was he getting a kiss.

Mrs Pochon, who had taught us for the latter part of our final year, was now relegated to scrawling on the blackboard by way of illustrating what he was telling us while waving his arms about like a madman.

He'd never taken the class before. But now, instead of talking about our futures, or playing games, like we had been all week, we spent our very last morning learning how to use apostrophes. It was as though it had somehow been forgotten and we couldn't possibly leave school without it. We had to pretend to concentrate really hard.

Thank's for that, teachers', Ive alway's said its' a gods'end.

Then we had dinner in the canteen and all the teachers stood in front of us and took it in turns to say much the same few words while we tucked into some meat that was hard to identify followed by a lovely apple pie which one of the chubby dinner ladies had made us specially.

We were wonderful. We had great lives ahead of us. The school was very proud of our efforts. We were the future of the country.

Rest assured, we would never be forgotten. Nor would we ever forget Chaulden Juniors.

Back in my classroom, all 38 of us had to write our names and addresses (and a very few phone numbers) in a big brown address book so we could get in touch with each other via the school for ever and ever.

No one did. Ever or ever.

Next, we had to stand up and clap by way of wishing each other good luck in our new schools – we were split between four, all within a couple of miles. Cavendish School, Hemel Hempstead Grammar, Warners End Secondary Modern and Apsley Grammar, all of which became comprehensives in 1970.

Then we all filed out, got patted by the lovely, kind, white-haired Mrs

Pochon, strolled through the gates and went home.

Never even looked round. No fuss, no bother.

That's how it was.

"You're a big boy now, you have to stand on your own two feet and get to be a real somebody. But never forget one thing: once a toe rag, always a toe rag." That's what Granda said.

Granda knew everything in the whole world.

But even he knew nothing at all about The Woman Downstairs.

PRINTED AND BOUND BY:

Copytech (UK) Limited trading as Printondemand-worldwide,
9 Culley Court, Bakewell Road, Orton Southgate.
Peterborough, PE2 6XD, United Kingdom.